# Crossings

*Discipleship for the Brokenhearted*

Tanya Grubaugh

**About the Author**
Tanya Grubaugh lives with her husband and children in Northern California. She trained as a social worker and counselor and has spent the last decade homeschooling. This is her first book.

Contact Tanya Grubaugh at: crossings.2008@att.net

Crossings: Discipleship for the Brokenhearted
Copyright © 2009 by Tanya Grubaugh

Title page photograph by Kathi Massey © 2008
Cover design by Lisa Eneqvist © 2009

ISBN 978-0-578-01263-6

All rights reserved. No part of this book may be reproduced or transmitted in any form or by any means, electronic or mechanical, including photocopying, recording, or by any information storage and retrieval system, without permission in writing from the author.

Unless otherwise noted, all Bible references are from the New International Version, © Zondervan Publishing. Used by permission.

Scripture taken from The Message. Copyright © 1993, 1994, 1995, 1996, 2000, 2001, 2002. Used by permission of NavPress Publishing Group.

Granada Press
California

# Acknowledgements

Friends and family have come alongside me as I've pursued the writing of this book, and I owe them a tremendous debt of gratitude.

To those who poured great time and effort into every page of this book, thank you for contributing your unique brand of expertise: Vicki Newman, thanks for all the editing and for all you taught me as a writer; Brad Franklin, thanks for talking through spiritual truths with me and for encouraging me to grow in my relationship with God through this project and always; Kim Fredrickson, God uses you as a great healer of hearts – thank you for all you've done for me personally and for working through the healing issues in this book; Kevin and Sally Melton, you encouraged me from the beginning, and you helped me keep the project on the front burner by consistently asking about it and reading through it. I needed that kind of kick start. You are all dear friends.

Over the years it took to write "Crossings," there were numerous people who helped me along the way. You've prayed for me, mentored me, shared your stories, read and edited portions of the manuscript, offered valuable suggestions for how to improve it, encouraged me to keep going, used "Crossings" in groups and with individuals and for yourselves. Thanks to Kathi Massey, Kelly Broughton, Jaqueline Ramsay, Barbara Straub, Karen Engle, Anna Morgado, Susan Mentink, Kathi Sturgeon, Jan Whitfield, Marlene Woertz, Teddi Pettee, Karen Tucker, Steve and Wende Seely, Don and Faye McFarland and others.

Thanks to Lisa Eneqvist for her graphic design work on the cover.

Thank you to Colleen DeAngelis and Eve Hayward, who were willing to be guinea pigs in my first "Crossings" small group using an early version of the book. Your gracious and constructive feedback after 10 weeks together was invaluable.

For getting early groups off the ground, thanks to Cynthia Fehrenbacher and Diane DeCarlo and the whole Bayside group. Thanks to Patty Record, Nancy Atchley and all the women at Powerhouse Ministries in Folsom. You rock!

To Jami Spencer, who inspired me to write this study – God spoke through you so many times. Thanks for believing in me.

To my children, who have been a huge inspiration – when I grow up, I want to be just like you. Thanks for encouraging me to finish. Thank you for enduring all the times I sat at the computer for long stretches.

To my husband Karl – you have lived this book with me. You fill me with confidence. Your love has helped me grow. You've read and re-read every word. You are a brilliant editor and sounding board. You are a gift to me.

# Contents

| | | |
|---|---|---|
| Introduction | | 7 |
| How to Use Your Book | | 8 |
| Chapter 1 | Crossings | 11 |
| Chapter 2 | Broken Trust, Broken Heart | 19 |
| Chapter 3 | Knowing God's Heart Through His Word | 29 |
| Chapter 4 | Healing the Broken Heart Through Prayer | 39 |
| Chapter 5 | Guilt – Longing to be Known and Loved | 49 |
| Chapter 6 | Shame – Alienation That Breaks the Heart | 63 |
| Chapter 7 | Fear – Losing Sight of His Presence | 77 |
| Chapter 8 | When God Waits | 91 |
| Chapter 9 | Home – The Promise of God With Us | 101 |
| Afterword | | 107 |
| Biblical References | | 108 |
| For Further Study | | 109 |
| Getting Support & Book Recommendations | | 110 |

# Introduction

God is a relentless healer of hearts, and He wants to heal yours.

For many years now, God has led me on a journey of healing my broken heart. He's always been a gentle physician and, although I've not always been a compliant patient, He's never given up on me.

I've felt the sting of condemnation from those who were meant to treasure me but couldn't. I've felt alone and inadequate. I've been betrayed by friends. But, over the years, God has taught me how to grieve losses and lean into Jesus for His healing touch. He's taught me how suffering, when attended to rather than pushed aside, can be integrated into my life to become a display of His power. I owe Him a great debt. I owe Him my life.

He never tires of my needs and He refuses to give up on my heart. No one else can claim such fortitude. No one else has such amazing determination, but then no one else is driven by such a great love.

In my walk with Him, God has shown me two things:
- how little I understand His heart toward me when I suffer
- how little I know about reaching out to Him and finding help when I hurt

I want to understand these things more clearly.

Perhaps your story is like mine – perhaps you, too, have been wounded and need God's touch. Maybe you want to understand His heart toward you in the middle of guilt, shame, fear or loss.

By reading this study and working through the accompanying questions, you're embarking on a journey to discover God's heart when you hurt and learn how to reach for Him in the midst of suffering. It's discipleship for the broken-hearted; a journey for brave souls because, although this is a task worth doing, it's not easy.

You and I live in a world that hands out as many bruises as there are grains of sand. We've been wounded, and we carry a broken heart with us into our world until we let the Healer of Broken Hearts mend it. My prayer is that, through these pages, God will begin to mend your heart and free you from guilt, shame and fear. I pray you'll learn how to reach out to Him and be comforted by Him when you hurt. Most of all, I pray you'll learn the truth about His heart, catch a vision for the significant role you play in His story, and thoroughly believe Him when He says you are precious in His sight.

Be strong and courageous, for God is with you. He will never leave you nor forsake you, for He is a relentless healer of hearts. And He wants to heal yours.

> *The Spirit of the Sovereign Lord is on me, because the Lord has anointed me to preach good news to the poor. He has sent me to bind up the brokenhearted, to proclaim freedom for the captives and release from darkness for the prisoners ...*
>
> *Isaiah 61: 1*

# How to Use Your Book

In many ways, I feel completely unprepared to write about how God can redeem us from being brokenhearted. Matters of the broken heart are so very complex. In fact, I think I could write again every few years and, having grown spiritually and emotionally, I would find the process – and the product – entirely different, more mature, more honest.

But not to begin means I would have failed to write this book at all. So please know that I write not with all the answers but as a fellow traveler. My hope is that I will honestly and sensitively walk this path with you.

This is by no means a complete discussion of the issues surrounding the brokenhearted. It is only intended to be a starting point. This is not meant to be a study on the nature of suffering, only a study on how to reach out to God when you are suffering. This book attempts to answer the questions, "How does God feel about us in our suffering?" and "Can we reach out to Him and find help when we hurt?"

If you finish this study and are looking for more, the books and resources listed at the end might be helpful.

First, some definitions:

The term "heart" refers to the whole self – mind, emotion, will, hopes and dreams. The New International Version Study Bible says the heart, in the Bible, is "the center of the human spirit, from which spring emotions, thought, motivations, courage and action …" The writer of Proverbs says, "Above all else, guard your heart, for it is the wellspring of life." (Proverbs 4:23)

The "brokenhearted" refers to those who are hurting emotionally from a loss or a wounding. Those who are "crushed in spirit" are brokenhearted.

Being brokenhearted, however, isn't all bad. If you let God use it to remind you of your dependency on Him and your need to connect with others, brokenness can build a strong, humble, healthy soul. Our broken heart can drive us to defensiveness, blame and isolation, or it can steer us toward closeness with God and others.

Here are some other suggestions that will help you get the most from this study:

- Leaders, seriously consider keeping your group small – six or fewer. Smaller groups give authenticity and safety a chance to thrive. Sometimes people need to talk for a while, but they will hold back if they feel there are too many others needing to be heard.
- Leaders should read through the study and maybe even work through it themselves before leading a group through it. (You might appreciate the advance warning!) Give yourself time to heal and work through your own issues that come up. It's like the flight attendant's recommendation on commercial airliners – "Parents, adjust your oxygen mask first before helping your children with theirs." If you want to help others, remember to first seek help yourself. You'll be far more sensitive and ready to hear others' pain if you do.

- When planning out the number of weeks for a group study, consider taking two weeks each for Chapters 5 and 6. The questions for these chapters are split into two sections for that purpose. Groups that want to cover these chapters in a single week can certainly do so, however, so go with what works for your group.
- When verses or phrases leap off the page, sit with them. Sit with your pain and let God enter there. Stay with the thought, the grief, the anger for a little while and listen for God in it.
- When you feel resistance to digging deeper, try listening to music. Music has a way of entering the soul when other things can't. If music doesn't work for you, maybe something else will. Maybe you need candles or a walk in a beautiful spot or talking about your resistance with a friend who will just listen. What does your heart need in order to go deeper?
- Journal! Do it late at night if God speaks to you then. God opens us up when we write, and we make important connections and solidify promptings. But if writing doesn't work for you, find another way to chronicle your journey. Read and think about the questions and then tell a friend or mentor what you learn; walk and talk to God about it; say it into a recorder; draw pictures – anything that helps get it out from the inside.
- Share! Talk about what you're learning in this study with others, because when you share you connect with God by connecting with His children. That's one of His healing methods. I encourage you to find a group for this journey. You might like to use the group discussion questions at the end of each chapter or you might choose your own questions to lead your discussion. Either way, make it work for your group.
- Working through "Crossings" on your own can be valuable, too. Talk to a trusted friend, counselor or mentor about the things you're experiencing. Others can spot things you might miss. They can encourage you when you want to stop and they can be with you in your suffering. God uses others to heal us.
- Choose one thought, plan or verse from each chapter that most stands out to you so you don't get lost in a sea of ideas. God wants your mind clear and unhurried, free of noise and constant distraction. Choosing one thought especially significant to your heart can calm the storm.
- Pray! Pray for yourself, and ask others to pray for you. This is incredibly important. Listen to your heart and God's heart. Ask Him what He's hoping for you on any given day. Ask Him what's on His mind. And take time out to ask yourself what you're feeling, what you're thinking, what you're hoping for. Your feelings, your will, your mind and your passions all need your attention in order to heal.

Mending the heart is a lot like spiritual growth – it has to happen in God's time, by His prompting, with the involvement of others and in light of the way He's wired you up. We heal when we honor our heart by acknowledging its suffering, when we reveal that suffering to God and others and when we receive their love.

Healing takes time, patience and hard work. But you are in good hands. And you can rest knowing that, if you miss anything significant the first time, Jesus will bring the opportunity around again.

May God grant you "power, together with all the saints, to grasp how wide and long and high and deep is the love of Christ…"

# Chapter 1
# Crossings

*Now then, you and all these people, get ready to cross
the Jordan River into the land I am about to give them.*
                                                *Joshua 1:2*

When I first met Jesus, I was a teenager – and I desperately needed to know I mattered. I busily went through the motions of my adolescent life, but inside, I felt the pain of inadequacy, loneliness and insignificance. I preferred to think of my pain as a passing adolescent hang-up, but now I know I would have carried the burden to my grave. When the hubbub of schoolwork, time with friends, student government and basketball games was done, and I was alone and quiet, one question haunted me: "Does it really matter that I'm here at all?"

One night during those high school years, two of my best friends burst into my bedroom full of laughter. They were playing a game, and their mission was to kidnap friends and take them to our high school's Campus Life/Youth for Christ meeting. I was reluctant to go, but they prodded me and I soon found myself sitting among a throng of teenagers playing crazy games and hearing about Jesus in a whole new way. That night I began the life-long process of understanding how I personally matter to Jesus, the maker of the universe, the Builder of Bridges.

That was my first crossing – from life on my own to a life with the God who loves me.

***

But I had developed some unhealthy beliefs about myself and some unhealthy ways of coping. Crossing over to a life with God doesn't magically make all those old ways disappear. I carried all that baggage right along with me.

One of the pieces of luggage was shame. Shame told me I could never measure up and I had nothing to offer. Another piece of that baggage was fear. Fear told me I better not take risks or my inadequacy and shame might be discovered.

I stumbled through my college years, longing to be confident, worthy and lovable. I treasured no dreams or passions. My heart was broken, and I was too afraid to reach out to God and the people who could help me mend it.

When I married at 22, I was clueless about how my broken heart affected me and my relationships. Often, one simple event or some innocent comment from my husband set off a whole flood of heartache. I thought he was the one who was wrong, but my heart needed mending. I was too afraid to tell my husband about my heartache, so I pretended it didn't exist. That only made matters worse, and so we stumbled through our early married years.

I needed healing, but I shoved down the pain instead of feeling it and opening up to God and others. I tried to silence my heart, and I went through the motions of church activities with only moments of passion for my savior. I felt like I was on the outside looking in on the close friendships others enjoyed. It wasn't the greatest place to be, but at least it was familiar.

Silencing my heart didn't make the pain go away. It only increased my isolation and confirmed my shame. But God is all-good and all-powerful. He doesn't let us suffer in vain. He uses pain for redemption, drawing us out of unhealthy, albeit familiar places.

And so He used my heartache to woo me back to Him. He gently helped me see the damage I'd inflicted on myself and my relationships. For the sake of avoiding pain, I'd closed out God and everybody else. I'd silenced my heart into deadness. The only way out was to let the pain surface.

Ready to make another crossing, I turned to God and said, "God, whatever it takes to draw me close to You, do it. If I have to look stupid or give up something important, whatever it is, I'm willing. Even feeling the pain of life has to be better than this deadness. Heal my heart and cause me to live for You again, whatever it takes."

This crossing was more difficult than the first because I had to feel all the pain I'd pushed away for years. And I had to be vulnerable enough to reveal my shame, my fear and my broken heart to God and others.

That was my second crossing – from silencing my heart to giving it a voice and integrating my brokenness into a deeper, more honest relationship with people and with the God who heals me.

*** 

The Israelites of the Old Testament knew about crossings. They experienced a few of their own. For more than 400 years, the Israelites were slaves in Egypt. With every new generation, the crushing weight of abuse and captivity grew heavier, as did the despair.

And so the people cried out to their God, and God heard their pleas. He sent Moses to lead them to freedom. And after many displays of God's power, and not a little strutting of Pharaoh's stubborn heart, Pharaoh finally released the Israelite slaves and they went out rejoicing.

But there's a lot of back and forth to this story. Once Pharaoh saw what he lost, he changed his mind. No deal. He and his army raced out to the desert to retrieve their slaves.

By now the Israelites were camped near the sea. When they saw Pharaoh's army coming after them, they quickly forgot their 400 years of suffering. They turned on Moses, blaming him for leading them to this so-called freedom. They claimed they would rather be slaves in Egypt than risk dying in the desert. As Pharaoh drew nearer, they busied themselves with writing their Egyptian epitaphs: "Here lie Joe and Josephine Slave. They decided freedom was too risky."

But God is all about choices. He offered the Israelites two options – a return to slavery in Egypt or a crossing on dry ground through the middle of the sea. God told Moses to raise his staff, and the waters parted. The people quickly accepted the sea-crossing deal, and more than 600,000 men and their families safely crossed over to a new life.

Like the Israelites, you have an offer on the table. God wants much more for you than you can imagine. He came to bind up the brokenhearted, to set the captives free and to release prisoners from darkness. He wants you to experience a healing of your heart that only His Truth and Love can bring. For this to happen, you must make a crossing from your side of the sea, the slavery of your past and your ways, to His side, the freedom of His future and His purposes.

Be warned. This is no easy process. It will be difficult. You'll want to stay right where you are.

Looking back to my childhood, I remember my father as an intimidating giant of a man. His unpredictable anger and criticism scared me into hiding and laid a foundation of fear that stuck with me into adulthood. As the years passed, my father became old and frail, but I continued to fear him. In fact, I became fearful of most men, avoiding them at work, at church, even at the grocery store. For many years I remained in that place of fear because stepping out of my hiding place was too frightening. It took a lot of determination, a deep trust in my Heavenly Father, and opening up to others to move beyond fear to a place of healing and freedom.

Do you need to know you're not alone and that it matters that you're here? Does your heart need to be heard? My prayer is that, in time, you'll find – as I have – that you can cross from life on your own to a life with a God who loves you, and that this God is a ready and able Healer, a Builder of Bridges.

At the end of C. S. Lewis' book, "The Voyage of the Dawn Treader," the great lion Aslan makes a final appearance. The children have come to the end of the Narnian world, at the edge of Aslan's country. Lucy, one of the children who originally stumbled into Narnia, asks Aslan: "Will you tell us how to get into your country from our world?"

"I shall be telling you all the time," said Aslan. "But I will not tell you how long or short the way will be; only that it lies across a river. But do not fear that, for I am the great Bridge Builder."

Trust God to build a bridge for you. You won't be disappointed.

*Trust God from the bottom of your heart; don't try to figure everything out on your own.*
*Listen for God's voice in everything you do, everywhere you go; he's the one who will keep you on track!*
*Proverbs 3:5-6, The Message*

# Write Your Story

*I don't want to leave here. I don't want to stay, it feels like pinching to me either way.*

*The places I long for the most are the places where I've been. They are calling after me like a long lost friend ...*

*The past is so tangible, I know it by heart, familiar things are never easy to discard.*

*I was longing for some freedom, but now I hesitate to go. I am caught between the promise and the things I know.*

*I've been painting pictures of Egypt, leaving out what it lacked. The future feels so hard and I want to go back.*

*But the places that used to fit me cannot hold the things I've learned, and those roads were closed off to me while my back was turned.*

*"Painting Pictures of Egypt,"*
*Sara Groves, from the album "Conversations"*

Singer and songwriter Sara Groves has given a voice to what I so often feel about change and healing. No matter how good the healing can be, it's still uncomfortable, so unfamiliar. Whether we're setting tougher boundaries with others, learning to reach out for help or just beginning to open up about a painful past, change is hard. We're like the Israelites, wanting to return to what we know, "…painting pictures of Egypt, leaving out what it lacks."

But returning to the familiar for us is also like a return to Egypt for the Israelites. It's a return to bondage. Failing to reach out to others for help continues the bondage of isolation. Not setting limits on others' abusive behavior toward us breeds the bondage of victimization. Remaining silent about a painful past keeps us bound to repeating the patterns of that past.

So how are you feeling about this journey of healing? Below are some questions to help you process what's happening in your heart. The scriptures can give voice to what you may be feeling. I encourage you to express yourself freely. It's the first step to healing and engaging with God.

## Day One – Looking Ahead

1. Which statement do you relate to best?
    - I need to know I matter
    - I need to know I'm not alone
    - I need to stop silencing my heart
    - I need to make some kind of crossing I just don't know what it is yet
    - I need to make another kind of crossing

2. Read Exodus 14:5-31. What brokenness makes up your own personal "Egypt?" What do you want to leave behind?

3. Broken hearts go with broken dreams. Maybe you have an:
    - undeveloped or underdeveloped gift that others scoffed at
    - a goal you've held since childhood that seems unattainable
    - a personality trait or behavioral pattern you thought you could have overcome by now

    Which of your dreams was broken along life's way?

## Day Two – Help From God

1. How do you feel about trusting God with your heart so He can help you make a crossing?

2. Healing our broken heart is part of the "good work" God is doing in us. Look up Philippians 1:6 and describe what the writer says about that work.

3. What is the good work God began in your heart?

## Day Three – Help From Friends

1. What support will you need from others as you move through this study? Will you need others to listen to you? Will you need someone to help you with tasks so you can get some time to yourself? Be specific.

2. God designed us to experience love, truth and grace through others. You need others in your life. Look up Romans 12:15, 1 John 4:7, and Ecclesiastes 4:9-12. What do these scriptures say about helping one another? Who rejoices with you or mourns with you? Who picks you up when you fall down?

### Day Four – Crossings Defined
1. Crossings are anything that move you closer to God or others. Examples of crossings are: believing God gave you gifts and talents and wants you to use them, recognizing when you're afraid and reaching out to God for help, revealing your guilt or shame to trusted others. A crossing can be a new step of belief or transformation. What crossing do you need to make?

2. What's the most helpful thought you came across in this chapter? Which scripture could you carry with you for the weeks ahead?

*Dear Jesus,*
*This new step is launching me into unknown territory. I need you to be with me in a clear way. Help me trust that you know what you're doing.*
*You made the universe and you made me, and some say that should be enough for me to trust you. But sometimes that's just not enough. Help me every step of the way and give me friends to lean on through the process.*
*Show me how much you love me today. And thank you.*
*Amen*

**Group Discussion –** *How can God and others help you cross over from hurt to healing?*

1. What part of the study made the biggest impression on you this week?

2. How can others help you right now? (Read 1 John 4:7)

3. We've all been broken. What brokenness hurts the most right now?

4. What healing do you need? What do you need to believe about yourself? What transformation do you need in your heart? In short, what crossings do you need to make?

5. Which verse is most helpful to you from this chapter?

# Chapter 2
# Broken Trust, Broken Heart

*But we trusted that it had been he who would have redeemed Israel: and besides all this, to-day is the third day since these things were done. (Luke 24:21, Noah Webster version )*

It all hinges on trust.

When my husband Karl was 23, his younger brother was killed in a car accident. Kyle was always full of laughter and adventure. Losing him was devastating, and Karl wondered if he could trust God's heart in the middle of this tragedy.

Today, Karl says the thing that gave him the most hope was what a friend wrote to him in a note. It was from Romans 8: "…neither death nor life, neither angels nor demons, neither the present nor the future, nor any powers, neither height nor depth, nor anything else in all creation will be able to separate us from the love of God that is in Christ Jesus our Lord."

There are questions Karl has never had answered about his brother's death, but the thing he needed most at the time was made clear in that passage: God loved him and He loved Kyle. None of that changed when Kyle died. Karl's belief in God's unfailing love helped him walk through that dark time.

Sometimes life hurts, and trusting God is hard. He knows life can hurt. But as writer Eugene Peterson says, "He's here, and He's on your side."

\*\*\*

The Book of Luke tells us the story of how two of Jesus' followers stopped trusting in God's heart. The story begins after Jesus was killed, buried and came back to life.

Jesus has a talent for meeting people right where they are. So, on this day, He went for a walk with two men on their way into Emmaus. When Jesus joined them along the road, they didn't recognize Him. They didn't yet know, or believe, He was alive again. And after all, how often do you bury someone and three days later, there they are walking and talking with you on your way to town?

Unaware they were speaking to Jesus, they told Him the story of how they believed He would be their hero. "…we trusted that it had been he who would have redeemed Israel." They thought a divine savior would free them from the oppressive Romans. But, they said, He had been brutally killed. (I wonder if Jesus was smiling at the irony of being the only person to discuss his own death after experiencing it.)

These followers of Christ felt bewildered and defeated. What hope was there for the future? Their redeemer lay in a tomb, dead. They probably asked themselves questions like: "Who was this Jesus, really? Why didn't He use His God-power to wipe out those who were about to kill Him? If Jesus loved us, why did He abandon us?"

"We trusted..." they said. Past tense. Their hope died when Jesus died.

These men had no clue what God was up to when He died on the cross. Figuring it was all over, they reasoned Jesus was crazy or, worse, just a liar. But in their moment of doubt, Jesus was in the middle of the greatest rescue operation the world would ever know.

Jesus went to the cross full of love and determination. It was His Father's plan. Jesus' death was the one thing that could buy back our lives. He suffered for us, His life for our life. Redemption.

And, Jesus' death on the cross was God's plan for suffering *with* us. God didn't want to be some distant, unsympathetic spirit. He became one of us to experience our pain and to demonstrate He's with us in it. What profound love! "But God put his love on the line for us by offering his Son in sacrificial death while we were of no use whatever to him." (Romans 5:8, The Message)

God had a much bigger plan than His followers could ever dream up. But Jesus' friends didn't see it. Nobody saw it.

\*\*\*

Like the two men from Emmaus, we look at God through the lens of our circumstances and then misunderstand His heart. When we suffer, we want to know where God is, and sometimes, many times, He seems absent.

Our ability to trust God was broken the first time humanity rebelled against Him. Our trust in Him is broken, and so our hearts are broken. When we're hurting and we can't see God, instead of assuming He's here helping us, we automatically assume He's left us. We ask, "Is God dead or only powerless? If he loves us, why does He abandon us?"

I've been a mother for more than 17 years now. Ever since my children were babies, I had a long-term vision for them. The problem is they came with their own agenda, mainly consisting of "No, no, no! Mine, mine, mine!" and "I do it!" Whew! Those were some trying times.

> *He (the Spirit of God) knows us far better than we know ourselves...and keeps us present before God. That's why we can be so sure that every detail in our lives of love for God is worked into something good.*
>
> *Romans 8:27-28, The Message*

Once, when my resourceful daughter Lauren was a toddler, she got hold of a kitchen knife. It was tricky taking it away from her because she was determined to keep it and she was holding onto the sharp end of it. I couldn't just yank it out of her hand, but I had to take it from her. She held her ground, but I eventually pried her little fingers off it. Oh, did she scream! Thankfully, she wasn't hurt – she just wanted the knife back.

Children don't understand that loving parents train and protect them. Because of their love for their children, parents focus on the big picture. Mothers and fathers see a child's current and future needs and have some ideas about how to meet those needs. They try to communicate to their children that – although they love them immensely – this isn't a happiness-at-all-costs operation. Parents keep children from danger because they know the potential for injury. A child, however, has a completely different agenda. She would prefer to have the dangerous, razor-sharp knife back, thank you very much.

We find it hard to trust God because, like children, we don't see the whole picture. But He has bigger dreams for us than we can imagine.

His primary motive in all things is love and redemption. And so, ever since humanity first turned its back on Him, God has been focusing His power on drawing us back to Himself. Because of His immense love, He brings a deeper healing, a bigger freedom, a restoration of the heart. Nothing can separate us from His love, and He will never give up on His vision for us to know that.

Sometimes life hurts, and trusting God with tremendous heartache might feel impossible. At those times there is nothing we can do – we can only be. And even that is a deep trust.

> *Trust isn't pretending not to be afraid. It's being afraid, and letting yourself be loved.*

He doesn't ask us to push the pain aside and pretend to be happy. "Don't worry, be happy" is not His lyric. Instead, this is His song: "Trust me because I love you, and my love is unchanging and never-ending. I'm here, and I'm on your side."

> *'Though the mountains be shaken and the hills be removed, yet my unfailing love for you will not be shaken nor my covenant of peace be removed,' says the Lord, who has compassion on you.*
> *Isaiah 54:10*

# Write Your Story

God is loving and good. He doesn't bring suffering into our lives; humanity has managed that well enough on its own. Suffering is either self-inflicted, brought on by others or brought to us from evil in the world. God takes our pain and uses it to redeem us like only He can. He's here, and He's on your side.

**Day One – Opening Up to Trust**
1. We all have some difficulty trusting God. What do you have trouble trusting God with – finances, relationships, reaching out to others for help, taking a risk with a talent or skill?

2. A young friend of mine has experienced the deaths of several significant people in her life. She believes God cannot exist, or, if He does, He must not love her. Read Mark 9:14-27. When is trusting God easy? When is it hard?

3. Emotional wounding creates huge obstacles to trusting. What experiences have you had that make trusting Him hard?

> *We suffer because it is this world, not some dream world that we would like to have, some utopia that we may fantasize about and wish to live in. We live in this world – after the Fall, this side of Eden, this paradise-lost world where sin entered by the choices of God's children. In this world, where now, instead of God's perfect and intentional will, we often – perhaps always – have to settle for His permissive and conditional will.*
>
> "Healing for Damaged Emotions"
> *David A. Seamands*

## Day Two – How Trust Grows

1. When we're vulnerable with others and find we're loved and accepted we learn God also is trustworthy. God uses others to help us heal and learn to trust. For example, if we've been abused as children, He may send us trustworthy people to help us learn that trusting others can be safe. How do you feel about revealing your broken heart to others?

2. Learning to trust requires some significant processes. In the first year of life, children need to bond to their parents or caregivers and develop a sense of attachment, belonging and safety. Then, as they grow, they need to learn healthy separation from those they love. If either of these processes fail, children struggle with trust. Describe your early years. Did you feel safe with your parents or caregivers? Were you able to say "no" without being abandoned emotionally or physically?

3. Healthy boundaries are essential to trusting others. If you continually open your heart to others who hurt you, you'll continually feel that others are untrustworthy. Do you discern well whom to trust? Do you need to grow in this area? What's your track record in this area?

4. Likewise, if you haven't been opening up to others it will seem foreign and uncomfortable. You might feel sensitive to others' responses even if they're gentle. That's what happens when we try something new. It's not that something is necessarily bad or wrong. How has this gone for you?

**Day Three – Evidence of a Trustworthy God**
1. What evidence is there that God can be trusted? List evidence from your life of God being trustworthy.

2. From these scriptures, write down signs of God's trustworthiness. What questions or doubts surface for you in these statements? Take your time. This is important.
    - *Psalm 23, Lamentations 3:22-23, John 10:11, John 14:6*

## Day Four – God's Promises

1. Read Isaiah 43:2-4. In this passage God is speaking to unfaithful Israel. What does God say Israel will have to endure? What does God promise Israel?

2. God doesn't always speak literally. Many times He speaks to us in metaphors. Not all the Israelites would have to walk through fire, for example, but they sometimes felt as though they were walking through fire. What have you endured that felt like walking through fire? What promises does God make to you? Ask Him about it.

3. You and I get confused about what God has promised us. Read 1 Corinthians 10:11-13. We often misread this verse as a promise that God won't let anything happen to us that we can't bear. But what is the subject of this passage?

> *Sometimes our misunderstanding of God is related to our definition of His goodness. Often we mistakenly define the goodness of God as what C.S. Lewis calls His "lovingness" or kindness. In his book, "The Problem of Pain" Lewis says this kind of goodness is driven by a happiness-at-all-costs plan. God is far more concerned with our long-term healing and drawing near to Him than our short-term happiness. To that end, He can use any and all circumstances for our greater good. And He does.*

4. Read John 16:33. What does it tell you? What conclusions can you draw about the trouble we'll have in this world?

**Day Five – The Ultimate Trust**

Often we assume God has somehow caused our pain or left us alone to get through it. But God is not the author of heartache, nor does He abandon us.

He longs for an intimate relationship with us. He stopped at nothing to win our hearts. When sin – our rejection of Him – put a great chasm between us, God sent His Son to bring us back to Himself. In "The Sacred Romance Workbook and Journal," John Eldredge tells the story of God's plan to win us back.

> *God creates us to live in his love. Our rejection of him breaks his heart. Still, he does not reject us. He sends his prophets to call us back to his heart. Finally he sends his only Son to die for us, to free us from the prisons of darkness and make us his own once more. God came at a great price to rescue us. He made a daring raid into enemy territory just to win you back.*

Because of the great chasm sin put between us and God, we need a bridge to cross over to Him. Jesus built that bridge. When you begin a relationship with Jesus, you cross that bridge and begin a new life – a life of following His ways instead of your own, a life of seeking Him and discovering your True self.

For some of you, this is the first time you've considered trusting God in a personal way. Or, perhaps you've known about God but you didn't know Him. He wants you to know Him personally. He wants a relationship with you.

1. If this idea of trusting God is new to you, please seriously consider it. Talk with Him about it. Talk with others who know Him. You can begin a relationship with God by choosing to follow Him and His ways. Thank Him for sending His Son, Jesus, to die for you, building a bridge back to Him. And then tell another follower of Christ so they can rejoice with you.
    - Read these verses. Romans 3:23, Romans 5:8, Romans 6:23, John 1:10-13. What do they mean to you? What do they tell you about Jesus Christ and yourself?

> *God does not open paths for us in advance of our coming. He does not promise help before help is needed. He does not remove obstacles out of our way before we reach them. Yet when we are on the edge of our need, God's hand is stretched out.*
>
> "Streams in the Desert"

2. When has God seemed absent from your life? When has He been present?

3. Read John 14:25-27, 15:9, 16:5-7. What evidence is there in these verses that God is here and He's on your side?

*Dear Jesus,*
*May I trust you as fully as I can while remaining in this human shell. Give me a trust in you that is based on faith instead of sight and set on you rather than my circumstances. I want to move mountains. I need to move some mountains. Please help me.*
*Amen*

## Group Discussion – *What happened to trusting God and others?*

1. What do you think of when you hear the word "trust?"

2. What's important to you from this chapter? Or what questions do you have?

3. What in your life is it hard to trust God with?

4. What experiences have you had that made it hard to trust God and others? What experiences have helped you learn to trust?

5. What step of trust do you need to make?

6. What evidence have you found in scripture and in life to back up God's trustworthiness? Read John 10:11, Psalm 23, Lamentations 3:22-23, John 14:6, Romans 5:8

# Chapter 3
# Knowing God's Heart Through His Word

*It was I who taught Ephraim to walk, taking them by the arms; but they did not realize it was I who healed them. I led them with cords of human kindness, with ties of love; I lifted the yoke from their neck and bent down to feed them.*
                              Hosea 11:3-4

*He sent forth His word and healed them.*
                              Psalm 107:20a

I had coffee with a friend of mine recently. As she shared with me, her sense of adventure and freedom bubbled over. She's beautiful and funny and a joy to be with. But life hasn't always been so free and adventurous for her.

Years ago, she was raped when she went on a date with a man from work. She became pregnant and had an abortion. She soon developed an intense fear of stepping outside her home. For a long time, she was chained by paralyzing anxiety, guilt and shame. She couldn't even go to God because she was sure He condemned her for the choices she'd made.

But God draws us to Himself despite the adversity that comes our way, and He drew my friend to His heart. Over the years, she's been in the process of healing. Her days aren't without struggle, but God has been gradually freeing her from the heavy weight of guilt and fear. She's crossed over to freedom. Now she has a powerful ministry to those who share similar stories.

So what, I asked her, enabled you to heal? Right away she answered, "Understanding God's true character."

From a young age, she learned about a punishing God. So after her abortion, she was wracked with feelings of condemnation. Only when she came to know the God who runs to us when we turn to Him did she begin to heal. "I needed to know He was safe to go to," she said.

\*\*\*

When we're hurting, we need to know God's character, to see Him as He truly is. We need to know He loves us and that His love is unshakable. In scripture we learn about God by studying how He interacted with people and what He said about Himself.

The Old Testament story of the Israelites, just released from slavery in Egypt, illustrates well the importance of knowing God. After setting the Israelites free, Pharoah changed his mind. He wanted them back. So Pharoah and his army went down to the sea to retrieve them. But as Israel watched the Egyptian army advance, God parted the sea so His people could cross to safety on the other side.

> *So he got up and went to his father. But while he was still a long way off, his father saw him and was filled with compassion for him; he ran to his son, threw his arms around him and kissed him.*
>
>                         *Luke 15:20*

I wish I could have been there to watch as the waters opened up for those newly freed souls. I would have loved to have seen the wonder and joy on their faces as they crossed the sea on dry ground.

But there's another part of the story I wonder about. After the sea crashed together again and the Israelites knew they were safe from their pursuers, I wonder what expressions they wore on their faces when they turned to gaze at the endless desert spread out before them. I bet they sighed a huge, collective, "Now what?"

I'm guessing their looks of joy turned to weary looks of despair. I bet they were a little disgruntled. Wouldn't you have the same reaction? You've been rushed to this vast desert that is your new, temporary home, and you didn't even bring your sunscreen, let alone food and shelter for the days ahead.

The problem was, the Israelites forgot, almost immediately after being freed from slavery in Egypt, that God was there and He was on their side. They were saved without knowing their savior.

Over the next 40 years, God provided food and water in the desert. He guided them with clouds and flames. He spoke to them. But they continued to distrust and defy Him. Over and over again, they complained that slavery in Egypt was far better than freedom in the desert. They held onto their slave mentality much tighter than they held onto their savior. Yet they were the apple of His eye, precious in His sight.

We and the Israelites share the same problem. We're afraid to trust God because we don't know His heart. But we are the apple of His eye. Just like Israel, we can be saved without knowing our Savior.

God knew we'd have this problem, so He gave us His Word, the Bible, to tell us about Himself. We need His Word, and lots of it. Without His Word as our guide, we not only get off track in our relationship with God, we aren't even on the same planet.

> *Now we see but a poor reflection as in a mirror; then we shall see face to face. Now I know in part; then I shall know fully, even as I am fully known.*
>
> *1 Corinthians 13:12*

God is about life and love, truth and grace. Without understanding Him, our picture of Him gets distorted. He becomes condemning, shaming, uncaring, untrustworthy, forgetful and deceptive as we fill in the blanks in our minds. If you aren't busy filling your mind with the truth about God, it will be filled with something else.

\*\*\*

It took me a long time to know God on an intimate level. Although I wasn't aware of it, my experience with my earthly father colored my perspective of a heavenly father. As a child, I felt unaccepted by my father. When I became a Christian, although I was thrilled to know God loved me, I unwittingly transferred my experience with a critical, earthly father to God. When I messed up, I believed God would hold that against me forever and set me on the shelf with all the other unworthy souls.

One Sunday, at a time when I felt I had really messed up, my pastor focused on Romans 8:1. It reads: "Therefore, there is now no condemnation for those who are in Christ Jesus." I'd read the verse dozens of times, but that morning my pastor asked a question that went to the heart of the matter: "If Jesus were walking in here with you to church today, what would He say to you?"

I imagined Jesus making a few choice remarks to straighten me out, a few caustic criticisms to correct my behavior. Then my pastor continued: "I believe He'd say something like, 'How's that situation going for you? I'm praying for you about that. Let me know how I can help.' "

It finally sank in. Jesus wasn't condemning me. He was offering to help. He paid too high a price – death on a cross – to then unfeelingly condemn me. Instead, He wanted to save and restore me.

I cried in church like never before as all the years of carrying this picture of a critical, condemning God washed away. I needed to know in my soul that God didn't condemn me but could be trusted. I needed to know who He is, and who I am to Him.

And I discovered Him in the scriptures, His story of my redemption.

*I will give them a heart to know me, that I am the Lord. They will be my people, and I will be their God, for they will return to me with all their heart.*
*Jeremiah 24:7*

> *...when people expose themselves to the pages of the Bible, something profound happens. They come into contact with the God of the universe and with the way he sees the world and us. Reading the Bible is one of the main ways God speaks to our lives and hearts. Although learning principles and truths is very important, coming close to God personally through the Bible is a higher value.*
>
> "How People Grow,"
> *Henry Cloud and John Townsend*

# Write Your Story

The people who cared for you when you were young laid one foundation for your life. Your beliefs about God and who you are to Him form another foundation. Knowing God's true character and who you are to Him is one essential aspect of healing your broken heart.

**Day One – Know Christ's Mission on Earth**

1. What is God like? Describe Him. What do you want to believe about Him?

2. We can get a glimpse into God's heart by knowing His passions and His mission. Read Isaiah 30:18 and Isaiah 61:1-2. (The passage in Isaiah 61 refers to Jesus.) Write a brief description of God's mission based on those scriptures. What did Jesus come to do?

3. Isaiah 61 says Jesus was sent to "bind up the brokenhearted". How might Jesus bind up your broken heart?

> *Let me put it this way: before we can love, we must know. We must know someone before we can love him. How shall we keep our "first love" for the Lord? By constantly knowing him better!*
>
> *"Practicing His Presence," Brother Lawrence*

## Day Two – Know God's Compassion

1. God is full of compassion. In fact, His heart for us is moved so readily that I wonder if He ever has to keep himself from acting on His compassion. Read this story about a funeral for a widow's son in Luke 7:11-17. What stands out to you about this story?

> *In a desert land he found him,*
>     *in a barren and howling waste.*
> *He shielded him and cared for him;*
>     *he guarded him as the apple of his eye,*
> *like an eagle that stirs up its nest*
>     *and hovers over its young,*
> *that spreads its wings to catch them*
>     *and carries them on its pinions.*
> *The Lord alone led him;*
>     *no foreign god was with him.*
>
>                   *Deuteronomy 32:10-12*

2. Picture the scene: A woman has just lost her only son and the last of her immediate family. Jesus sees her tears and He's filled with compassion. Describe Jesus' feelings at that moment. When Jesus sees the widow grieving, what does He do and say to her?

3. If He was to stand before you right now and say those same words, "Don't cry," how would you feel? What do those words bring up for you?

*If you want to believe God is compassionate but have trouble believing it, you might need to experience His compassion through others. We need others to be Jesus to us so we can believe what God says about Himself.*

## Day Three – Know God's Boundaries

Henry Cloud and John Townsend's "Boundaries" addresses some critical aspects of healing.

Cloud and Townsend compare boundaries to owning a home and a yard. You maintain your yard and water the lawn, but you wouldn't expect your neighbor to water your lawn. Nor should you be expected to water your neighbor's lawn. The maintenance of your yard is your responsibility and your neighbor's is his. He may ask you to water his lawn while he goes on vacation, and then you can decide if you can do that. But generally, his lawn is his responsibility.

Cloud and Townsend write: "Boundaries define us. They define what is me and what is not me. A boundary shows where you end and someone else begins, leading to a sense of ownership. We have to deal with what is in our soul (Prov. 14:10), and boundaries help us define what that is. The Bible tells us clearly what our parameters are and how to protect them, but often our family or other past relationships have confused us about our parameters."

Mending your broken heart will very likely need to include strengthening your boundaries. A good place to begin that process is to study our best boundary role model – God.

I used to think that because God is so loving, He would never say no to people the way I sometimes wanted to. I thought saying no to others, especially when they needed me, was selfish. And God would never be selfish.

> *Love from the center of who you are; don't fake it. Run for dear life from evil; hold on for dear life to good. Be good friends who love deeply; practice playing second fiddle.*
>
> *Romans 12:9-10,*
> The Message

People whose boundaries have been abused or weakened tend to think of God as having no boundaries. But without boundaries, God becomes either an extension of us or a wimpy doormat. He is neither.

1. Consider an example of God and Jesus setting boundaries. Read Mathew 10:11-16. What does Jesus instruct His disciples to do if a home is undeserving? If Jesus loves all people, how can He tell His disciples to leave some of them behind?

2. Read Romans 12:9. What is the advice here? Describe the character of a god who would suggest we live this way.

3. Have you ever thought of God having boundaries before? How do you feel about God setting boundaries?

## Day Four – Know Your Identity in Christ

Once you know a little about God's character, knowing your identity in Christ, can make all the difference.

1. From these scriptures, note what you mean to God, how He feels about you or what He does for you. I encourage you to take these verses and write them on cards. Attach them to your mirror, dashboard, desk, kitchen window, forehead (!) – anywhere you can be reminded of what you mean to Him.
    - Psalm 34:18

    - Isaiah 49:14-16

    - John 15:15

    - 1 Corinthians 6:19-20

    - Romans 8:1-2

    - Ephesians 2:10

> *We need neither art nor science for going to God. All we need is a heart resolutely determined to apply itself to nothing but Him, for His sake, and to love Him only.*
> *"Practicing His Presence," Brother Lawrence*

2. The above verses tell you who you really are, what God does for you and what you mean to Him. Which verse does your heart need to hear most? What crossing or new step of belief do you need to make to see yourself the way God sees you?

3. People don't grow or learn in isolation. It's one thing to know God on paper and it's another thing to know Him by experiencing Him through others. My mentors and others taught me about God's grace. My friend from this chapter learned about His compassion through a loving support group that lived out His grace to her. What might God want you to know about Him that you can't learn all alone? In what setting can you learn that?

4. Name one thing that's especially important to you from this chapter. Which verses popped out at you that you can memorize?

> *To the Jews who had believed him, Jesus said, 'If you hold to my teaching, you are really my disciples. Then you will know the truth, and the truth will set you free.'*
>
> *John 8:31-32*

*Jesus,*
*There's so much of you to know but I want to know you as you really are. I trust you to reveal yourself to me according to your timing. Help me always seek to know you more. And as I know you better, I pray I'll embrace you more in all I do and all that I am. Thank you that you want me to know you intimately. That's amazing to me. Let me in on your secrets, for I honor you.*
*Amen*

**Group Discussion –** *How can God use scripture to heal your broken heart?*

1. What stood out to you the most this week?

2. In the past, what have you believed about God's heart toward you in the middle of suffering?

3. If Jesus walked into the room with you today what would He have said to you?

4. What did you find in the scripture this week about God's character? Read Luke 7:11-17 and Matthew 10:11-16.

5. What part of God's character do you need to understand more clearly? What don't you "get" about Him?

6. Who are you to God? Read Psalm 34:18 and John 1:12.

# Chapter 4
## Healing the Broken Heart Through Prayer

*They dress the wound of my people as though it were not serious.*

*Jeremiah 6:14a*

A pastor sat in the doorway of his church trying to catch a breeze in the heat of the day. He watched as a woman came up the steps. Full of anguish and tears, she entered the sanctuary.

Once inside, she dropped to her knees and wept bitterly, pouring out her pain and her longing to hold a child of her own. "O Lord Almighty, if you will only look upon your servant's misery and remember me, and not forget your servant but give her a son, then I will give him to the Lord for all the days of his life…"

She was suffering greatly. This was a prayer so deep that only her heart could speak it. And so while she continued praying, her lips moved but her voice was silent.

Thinking she must be drunk, the pastor chastised her. He told her to get rid of her wine. But she explained herself to him: "I am a woman who is deeply troubled. I have not been drinking wine or beer; I was pouring out my soul to the Lord."

When he understood, he prayed a blessing of hope for her. Then she left and her face was no longer downcast.

*\* \* \**

This is the story of Hannah, an Old Testament woman. With abandon, she freely gave God all her emotion and all her dreams. Even though her suffering lasted for years, she continued pouring out her heart to God. She didn't harden her heart; instead, she remained receptive to her Heavenly Father even when it looked like things would never change.

Hannah did what I so often have trouble doing. I grow weary of praying persistently about things that never seem to change. I've prayed long and hard that God might help me overcome various fears, but I still have fears. I'm afraid of rejection. I'm afraid of deeper relationships with people, afraid I'll fail them, afraid they'll see my weaknesses and reject me. Even though I've prayed that God would set me free from my fear, I don't get the *zap* of newfound freedom I'm looking for. Eventually, I get discouraged and I'm tempted to close the door to Him.

But it's those persistent prayers that have built my trust in God the most. Like a treasure hunter, when I dig down the deepest and the longest, I get the most reward. When I focus on the specific troubled areas of my heart over a period of time, God gradually opens my eyes to opportunities for healing.

> *The Lord has promised good to me, His word my hope secures.*
>
> *He will my shield and portion be as long as life endures.*
>
> *From the hymn "Amazing Grace," John Newton*

Recently I met with my pastor, but doing so was a frightening prospect for me. For years, I avoided talking to people in authority, afraid they'd see through to my weaknesses and reject me.

I could have avoided the conversation this time. But God was offering me an opportunity to conquer my fear, the very thing I'd been asking God to do for so long.

It wasn't easy. I walked into my pastor's office trembling and trying to conceal it. I left, however, feeling understood, validated, no longer so fearful. I also witnessed God using a brother to help heal my wounds. And I realized I could have missed this gift of healing if I wasn't praying for it for all those years.

We get weary of praying when things never seem to change. It hurts to bring up painful things repeatedly. We'd much rather talk with a friend, go shopping, take a trip, watch TV, eat chocolate. (I'd rather even clean the house!)

But Jesus doesn't want us to gloss over our heartache, dressing our wound "as though it were not serious." Pouring our heart out to Him in prayer is exactly what He wants us to do even if we've done it before … a zillion times. When we pray persistently we learn that God listens to us. It's how we grow with Him and how He heals us. It's how we learn to trust Him. Without praying openly and honestly, we risk hardening our heart toward Him and others.

I notice another thing about Hannah's prayer – she was prepared to give up the very gift she was asking for. Offering her son to God before he was even born, she learned to hold loosely to her dream but tightly to the Giver of Dreams.

When we pray for healing, we need to hold loosely to the treatment process but hold tightly to the Healer. As patients, we need the Great Physician's guidance because often we don't know what we need for healing. We can pray for mending but allow God to prescribe the treatment.

Over the years, Jesus has been healing my broken heart but the mending process hasn't always taken the path I thought it should. I have a history of saying yes when I want to say no, and sometimes it's wreaked havoc in my life. I thought the best remedy for the problem was to ask God to steer me clear of the pushy people in my life. I didn't ask Him to address my inability to say no. I just wanted Him to clear a path.

God's treatment plan included surgery. I wanted a Band-Aid. God wanted me to stand up in my relationships and use the voice He'd given me. He wanted me to see that my feelings matter and my intuition could be trusted. He wanted me to set boundaries and tell others what those boundaries were. Steering others away from my path would never help me. Only God-prescribed changes in me could bring what I really wanted.

Although I fought with God on this one, He hung in there. I got into a Boundaries support group and began to understand the health and value of saying no when I need to. As I grew closer to the others in my group, I saw how God wanted to use them to support me to set boundaries. Gradually, I learned the wisdom of God's remedies and surrendered to His surgery. I've never felt more strong and free. And I rejoice in the work He's done in my heart.

*Right again, God.*

Hannah prayed repeatedly with all honesty and emotion. She surrendered to God's ways for her son long before he was born. Later, after Hannah weaned Samuel and left him in the care of the priest, she prayed again. This time it was a prayer of rejoicing – not so much for her son as for the One who gave him to her.

Freely pour out your burden to God, even if you have to do it a zillion times. Let loose of the treatment process. Just as He did for Hannah, God will hear your plea.

*I poured out my tears*
*And He held them in His hands.*
*I asked Him to speak*
*And He whispered a sunset.*

# Write Your Story

## Day One – The Heart of Prayer

"I am a rock," Paul Simon sings. "I am an island. And a rock feels no pain. And an island never cries."

When we're hurting, we tend to shut down our heart. We think: "If I just don't feel, don't have dreams, don't trust God or others, don't acknowledge my needs, don't hope … then I won't hurt."

Early in life, I learned to silence my heart as a protective device. Because I wouldn't let myself feel or hope, my conversations with God were dry. I couldn't cry with Him, so I couldn't laugh or rejoice with Him either. I was lifeless toward Him.

Prayer is first relational, an open exchange of thoughts and feelings. You need your heart in prayer with God. If anything will halt your conversations with God and stop your healing, it's silencing your heart.

1. Silencing the heart is the natural fallout of living on this earth. Describe a time when you silenced your heart, shutting down your feelings and thoughts. You'll know that you've silenced your heart if:
    - it's hard for you to express your needs to others
    - you have a hard time recognizing your needs
    - you isolate yourself
    - you persistently seek to control everything and everyone around you
    - you don't want to trust others
    - you tell yourself not to get your hopes up

2. The silencing of feelings, hopes and dreams doesn't spring up out of the blue. If you've shut down your heart, there's a reason. Can you think of painful experiences that have made it unsafe to hope or dream? What were the circumstances?

3. Sometimes we shut down our heart because we're afraid our stronger feelings won't be accepted by God and others; we're afraid of being too emotional. But sometimes, when emotions run high, we communicate more honestly with God. And Jesus, who we're called to imitate, freely expressed His emotion. In fact, He's the most emotional guy I've ever met! Read Mark 3:1-5, John 2:13-17 and John 11:33-35. What's been your picture of Jesus emotionally? And what picture do you get from these Bible snapshots?

*Jesus came to mend your heart and give you abundant life. Ask Him to help you uncover what keeps you from that abundant life. Be willing to pray about heartache and frustration as well as hopes and victories. And be on the lookout for signs of new life.*

## Day Two – Resistance to God

My daughter Lauren is in high school now. Over the years, I've prayed God would give her big dreams and, most of all, that He would show her He is a big God. I've prayed God would plant a hunger in her heart for Him.

Three years ago, she had the opportunity to go on a mission trip to Costa Rica. At 15, she would have been the youngest member of the group and, needless to say, Costa Rica is far from her mother in California! When she first asked, I had big hesitations. After all, she wasn't ready.

But Lauren kept quietly prodding and one day she said to me, "Mom, I really think God wants me to go to Costa Rica." Well! What is a mother to do with that?

Finally, I poured out my fears to God and heard Him gently say, "Daughter, Lauren's not the one who isn't ready. You aren't ready."

I recalled the many prayers I'd uttered concerning my children. I've prayed that they would know Jesus and love Him deeply. I've prayed they'd be free to take risks in their adventures with Him. I've prayed surrendered prayers.

But now, in effect, I was saying to my daughter, "Lauren, God loves you and I, your mother, have a wonderful plan for your life!" No deal. I finally allowed her to go and many of my long-held hopes for Lauren were met in that trip. Sometimes, in prayer, we need to hold loosely to our dream and more tightly to the Giver of Dreams.

1. Read James 4:3. What does this passage tell you about prayer? When have you prayed with a heart open to God's ways? When have you told God how to do things?

2. Resistance stems from trying to get control. People who get angry with others when they won't do what they want are trying to get control. People who clean house when they really need to cry on someone's shoulder are trying to get control. Often people seek to control because they fear what will happen if they don't. Do you find yourself trying to take control of things and people around you? What are you afraid might happen if you don't take control?

> *You (God) will keep in perfect peace him whose mind is steadfast, because He trusts in You.*
>
> *Isaiah 26:3*

3. Prayer is a conversation with God. We need to speak to Him as well as listen. Consider how you listen to others. That provides some good clues about how you're listening to God. How attentive are you when listening to others? How might that carry over when you listen to God?

4. Read Philippians 4:6-7. Tell God about your fear of giving Him control.

**Day Three -- How Did God Wire You Up to Pray?**
1. A friend of mine was seriously injured in an accident recently. I don't know how she'll recover. When it happened, I was able to pray at times, and other times I could only rest in my belief that God was with me and with my friend. Sometimes we're so overwhelmed by ongoing heartache or crisis that we can't even pray. At those times we can criticize ourselves for not praying, believing we're not among the faithful. But it might not be that we're resisting God so much as we're frozen by our circumstances, afraid and grieving. God knows that about us. And so He sends His Spirit. Read Romans 8:26-27. What does the Spirit do for you? What do God and the Spirit know? How can this passage help you?

2. When I pray for my friend, my prayers are an outpouring of all my longings for her wholeness. These prayers are not eloquent. They are rough, raw requests from a bleeding heart, and I know God embraces them. Hannah poured her heart out to God and her prayers were embraced as well. You can read the story in I Samuel 1:1-2:2. How can Hannah's model of prayer help you when you're hurting and want to reach out to God?

3. Perhaps Hannah's approach to prayer isn't helpful to you. There are many models. You can read Nehemiah's prayers in the book of Nehemiah and King David's prayers in the Psalms. The key is learning how God wired you up to love Him. That will reveal a lot about prayer.
    - Is your style traditional or more contemporary?
    - Are you talkative or quiet?
    - Can you focus by just talking or do you need a journal to write it down?
    - Are you inspired to pray when walking out in His creation?
    - Are you inspired inside a quiet room with a candle?
    - Do you talk all day to Him?
    - Do you need a specific block of time to talk with Him?
      Think about what helps you open up to a friend. That can give you clues. How has God wired you up?

## Day Four – Just Pray

*All bodily mortification and other exercises are useless except as they serve to arrive at union with God by love. I have well considered this and found that the shortest way to God is to go straight to Him by a continual exercise of love and doing all things for His sake.*

Brother Lawrence

1. What are you hoping for in your communication with God? Is there a crossing you've made in your perspective on prayer?

2. The whole point of following Jesus is love. We communicate with the people we love. Write a letter to God. Tell Him honestly how you're feeling about Him – angry, joyful, secure, frightened. Life is a mixture. Pour out your fears and your triumphs, your pain and your joy. If you can't write it, just say it. If something is stopping you from talking to Him, talk to Him about that. Tell Him what you long for Him to do for you. Also tell Him who you long for Him to be to you. Thank Him specifically for the things He's done for you. (Just the fact you're doing this study means He's drawing you to Him.) Praise Him for the good things you know about Him.

*Jesus,*
*I get locked up when I'm talking with you. Help me understand those things that keep me from deep conversations with you. Help me remember the simplicity of prayer and heal my broken heart through intimate conversations with you.*
*Amen*

**Discussion Questions –** *How can God use prayer to heal your broken heart?*

1. What do you want to remember from this week's study?

2. Have you been able to go to God in prayer when you're hurting? What helped or hindered you from praying?

3. How can you reach out to God in prayer when you're hurting? Read Hannah's story in 1 Samuel 1:1-2:2.

4. What help do you need to grow in prayer?

5. What do you need prayer for right now?

# Chapter 5
## Guilt – Longing to Be Known and Loved

*I tell you the truth, whoever hears my word and believes him who sent me has eternal life and will not be condemned; he has crossed over from death to life.*

*John 5:24*

*Jesus Christ didn't come into this world to make bad people good. He came into this world to make dead people live.*

*Ravi Zacharias*

She saw Him for the first time from a distance. As she walked through her Samaritan village to draw water from the well, she said to herself, "He shouldn't be there. I'm the only one who comes to the well during the hottest part of the day." She considered going back, but she'd already come this far in the heat – the heat of the sun, and the heat of stares from disapproving neighbors.

She made every effort to avoid people, but she could never avoid the guilt that plagued her. She constantly remembered the many men she'd been with; men who used her. She wanted out of these relationships, but she couldn't stop trying to quench her thirst for real love.

As she drew nearer, she could see He was a Jew. "What is He doing here?" she asked herself. "The Jews hate Samaritans. They go out of their way to avoid us." She put on her toughest exterior, trying to hide from Him.

She was just about to fill her water jar when Jesus startled her. "Would you give me a drink of water?" he asked.

His words hung there while a dozen thoughts raced through her head. Her culture had numerous, specific rules about who could interact with whom. This man was breaking all of them. And He kept on talking.

Although she'd never seen Him before, the things Jesus said made it abundantly clear that He knew her and knew her well. She'd been married and divorced five times, more than was morally acceptable, and the man she was currently with was not her husband. The revelation that Jesus knew all about it both startled and comforted her.

Jesus offered her things she'd never heard of before, things like "living water" – spiritual water to satisfy her thirsty soul. Jesus was not who she expected. He was more interested in bringing life to her heart than insisting

> *'I am the way and the truth and the life. No one comes to the Father except through me.'*
>
> *John 14:6*
>
> *Jesus answered, 'Everyone who drinks this water will be thirsty again, but whoever drinks the water I give him will never thirst. Indeed, the water I give him will become in him a spring of water welling up to eternal life.'*
>
> *John 4:13-14*

on her good behavior.

She'd built a lifestyle around avoiding others, and so she continued to avoid Jesus now. Outwardly she evaded His words and His eyes. But inwardly, she found Him more and more convincing.

Then He told her He was the Messiah, and she realized this was the Son of God who looked her in the eye and loved her. Abruptly, she left her water jar and ran back to the village.

And on her way back she greeted her neighbors saying, "Come, see a man who told me everything I ever did. Could this be the Christ?"

\* \* \*

What an incredible story. A woman goes to a well burdened with guilt, thirsty for love, and she leaves set free, overflowing with life. I'm grateful for the woman at the well. I know the sin in my life and how guilt breaks my heart. I'm grateful I can see Jesus mending the heart of another guilty soul.

I rejoice with this woman for her newfound freedom. But I'm puzzled by her excitement. She felt free to tell her neighbors, "Come see a man who told me everything I ever did." Why was she thrilled about Jesus knowing everything she ever did? Doesn't it make you squirm to think about a stranger knowing all there is to know about you? But she was happy to be known, warts and all.

Maybe the answer lies in Jesus' words and the look in His eyes. In their short conversation, she realized Jesus knew how guilt had broken her heart. He knew about the men in her life, and He wasn't softening his hope for her to have one man, her husband, in her life. But unlike her neighbors, He understood what created the thirst that kept her with all those men.

Jesus knew her and loved her completely. That's what made her happy to be exposed. Jesus – the Messiah, the God who made her – knew all about her and loved her.

The Samaritan woman probably had no idea how much guilt shaped her life. Guilt can shape our lives, too. It makes us feel judged by others, and we develop a dozen protective devices just to cope. We put up barriers to protect ourselves from God and others. But the harshest critic is the voice inside our heads.

> *I do not understand what I do. For what I want to do I do not do, but what I hate I do.*
>
> *Romans 7:15*

Often we want to stop doing wrong things, to stop sinning. But our thirst for love and significance, when not satisfied by a connection with God and others, drives us to different sources of satisfaction – prestige, sex, money, power, addictions and compulsions of every stripe.

Even our desire to silence our guilt leads us to more sin and resulting guilt. We get trapped in a cycle of sin and guilt, sin and guilt, more sin and more guilt. In our quietest moments, we long to be known and loved, but we feel so undeserving of that love.

Sometimes, when you look back at abortion, abuse, affairs, violence, alcoholism and on and on, your guilt can seem insurmountable. People have looked me in the eye and said, "Oh, but you don't know how deeply I've hurt others. How can I ever get over that?" I feel the wall of their guilt reaching to the sky, and I have no answers and make no guarantees.

I only know the healing I've seen in myself and others – impossible crossings made. I've seen people open up to one another and seek God's healing touch together. They will never forget their sin, but they learn to accept themselves as God does.

Only God has the answers. Only He can overcome the insurmountable. He doesn't ask you to get over it. But perhaps when you experience the forgiveness and acceptance of God and others, when you see that it's not about what you've done but about His nature, maybe then you can learn to forgive and accept yourself.

\*\*\*

Jesus gets it. He knows all about our sin and guilt and what they do to us. He knows all the wrong things we've ever done and all the wrong thoughts we've ever had, but He still loves us. He looks underneath our choices and sees our thirst for love and significance. He knows we're prone to sin, and He offers us Living Water that quenches our thirsty soul.

I pray you'll learn that He knows you completely and loves you deeply. Like the woman at the well, may you run free, shouting, "Come see a man who told me everything I ever did!"

*He heals the brokenhearted and binds up their wounds.*

*Psalm 147:3*

# Write Your Story

Someone once said to me, "I don't believe babies are born sinful." I understood what she meant. Babies don't come into the world with evil intent (although when they won't stop screaming at 2 a.m., you might be tempted to think otherwise.) Their cries come from a legitimate need, and those cries are God's way of getting parents to pay attention.

But give that sweet baby free reign as a toddler, and watch him turn into one selfish, domineering monster. I know. I've raised three of them. When they reached 1½, I knew I had my work cut out for me. I needed to train my children away from their natural self-centeredness or pay dearly for not doing so. They were prone to sin right from birth. We all are.

We know the good we ought to do, and we don't. We know the bad we ought to stay away from, and we won't.

Often we feel guilty when we've done something wrong. Some of our wrongdoing or sin is borne out of the years of battering we've experienced. We need help from God and others to heal and come away from that sin. Some sin results from our own rebellion. Either way, when we sin, guilt quickly follows. And long after we've changed our ways, guilt can haunt us.

Sin is a given in us, but we try to hide it anyway. Henry Cloud writes: "We must worship God in *relationship and in honesty*, or we do not worship him at all. The sad thing is that many of us come to Christ because we are sinners, and then spend the rest of our lives trying to prove that we are not!"

## Chapter 5 – Part 1
## Day One – Sin and Guilt Break the Heart

1. Like the Samaritan woman, our guilt keeps us from life – real, abundant life. Guilt keeps us from joy, peace, confidence, from using our gifts, from taking risks. What is your guilt keeping you from?
   - Trying out new relationships
   - Being vulnerable with those closest to you
   - Saying no to things you don't like
   - Feeling confident
   - Viewing your future with hope
   - Discovering your talents and using them
   - Feeling loved by God and others
   - Trusting yourself in the areas you've failed before

2. Read Romans 7:14-25. The author, Paul, is speaking openly about himself. What seems to be his trouble? What sin stems out of your naturally rebellious human nature? What do you struggle with and can't seem to do right? What have you struggled with in the past? Be specific.

3. Read John 4:1-26. A great emptiness led to the Samaritan woman's sin. Jesus knew that. She seemed to be looking for love outside of a relationship with God. What sin is tied to your emptiness? What sin results from years of pain or neglect someone inflicted on you? (For example, when we experience childhood abuse it can lead to violent anger, lack of forgiveness, revenge, medicating pain with drugs or sex.) Be specific.

4. What do you want to tell Jesus about your sin and the guilt you've felt? What do you want to hear from Him in return? What help do you need from Him and others to address your sin?

*When we know we need God, we're ready to receive grace.*

> *If sometimes I have no thought of God for a good while, I do not become disquieted because of it. But, after having acknowledged my failure to God, I return to Him with even greater trust since I was so miserable in having forgotten Him.*
>
> "Practicing His Presence,"
> *Brother Lawrence*

## Day Two – He Cancelled the Written Code Against Us

1. Read Exodus 12:1-13. What did God ask the Israelites to do? Why? Describe the Passover lamb.

> *Guilt keeps us focusing inward and on the past. Sorrow about our sin is transforming, drawing hearts together in love.*

2. Sin put up a mammoth-sized wall between us and God. But God always has and always will want an intimate relationship with us, so He provided a way to break down that wall. For the Israelites, God allowed the sacrifice of animals to cover the wrongdoing of Israel. Look up the word "atone" or "atonement" in the dictionary. Read Leviticus 16. The atonement process was graphic, involved and specific, and other sacrifices were required throughout the year. Describe that process.

3. The process of sacrificing animals never permanently broke down the wall. Read Hebrews 10:11-14, 1 Corinthians 5:7, Ephesians 1:7 and Colossians 1:20. What happened?

4. Today, Jesus is our Passover lamb and His sacrifice covers our sin once and for all. What do Hebrews 10:22 and Colossians 2:13-15 tell us happened to our guilt? And what does all of the above tell you about God's perspective on your sin?

## Day Three – People-pleasing Guilt

My pastor used to jokingly say, "Pack your bags. We're going on a guilt-trip!" We have mother-guilt, daughter-guilt, spouse-guilt, friend-guilt, God-guilt, church-guilt, waistline-guilt, guilt for wanting to stay at home with kids, guilt for wanting to work, guilt when we say "No."
Don't stop me now – I'm just warming up!

1. People-pleasing is another source of guilt. It's the kind of guilt you feel when you want to say "no" to someone but can't. It comes from trying to be perfect for God and others, and it comes from fear of rejection if we aren't perfect for God and others. As Christ followers, we're especially good at afflicting ourselves with this guilt. But Jesus came to rescue us, because no amount of goodness is good enough. And if goodness were the primary goal, our faith would look very different. What's the biggest source of your people-pleasing guilt? Who do you feel most guilty around? Read Romans 5:8. What does this verse tell you about God's heart toward the imperfect you?

> *We can't make ourselves be good anyway. Keith Green used to say that fruit trees can't force themselves to grow fruit. M-m-m peach! Instead, we need to rely on God to prompt changes in us, to help us grow with the support of his His people.*

2. If people in your past rejected or shamed you when you expressed your needs, you'll hear a harsh inner voice whenever you say what you want. What makes it hard for you to say "no" when you want to? What messages do you hear when you're considering saying "no"?

3. How happy are you about the responsibilities you've taken on? Do you ever feel resentful? About what? Be specific. Now read 2 Corinthians 9:6-7. What motivates you to give of yourself? And how does God want you to give?

Many of us struggle with people-pleasing. It's a huge guilt trap because you can never do enough and there are plenty of people ready to use guilt to get what they want from you. You can get so busy pleasing others that you lose yourself and what God has for you. If you struggle with saying "yes" when you really want to say "no," reading the book and discussing the workbook "Boundaries" by Henry Cloud and John Townsend might give you the insight and courage to break free of that pattern.

> *This righteousness from God comes through faith in Jesus Christ to all who believe. There is no difference, for all have sinned and fall short of the glory of God, and are justified freely by his grace through the redemption that came by Christ Jesus.*
>
> *Romans 3:22-24*

## Chapter 5 – Part 2
## Day One – The Voice of the Accuser

Jesus has left us in the care of the Holy Spirit. And one of His many tasks is to convict us of wrongdoing and draw us back to God.

But sometimes guilt moves far beyond conviction. Sometimes, you and I feel guilt for sins we've confessed and turned from long ago. This guilt is fueled by two voices – our own harsh inner voice (1 John 3:18-20) and the voice of condemnation from our enemy, Satan.

The people who cared for you and me as children weren't perfect. They had their own baggage then, just as you do now. When you act in ways opposed to their desires, whether they're with you or not, you'll hear the voice of guilt calling out to you. You also could have your own highly developed guilt-voice trying to keep you in line. Living up to those voices can lead to depression, resentment and a host of fears.

The devil also has an agenda for you. Satan knows if he can convince you that it's God who condemns you, you'll remain far from God's heart. If Satan can defeat you by laying on a heavy burden of guilt for sins long-ago confessed and forgiven, he will.

It's critical that you understand the difference between the loving conviction of God and the condemnation coming from within and from Satan.

1. God knows the wrong you've done. And He's already paid the price for it. He has no need or desire to condemn you. But you have an enemy. Read Revelation 12:9-10, John 8:44 and 1 Peter 5:8. After reading these passages, describe Satan's character and personality.

2. For 20 years, I believed God condemned me for my sin. But when I realized the concept of God condemning me wasn't Biblical, it occurred to me there must be another source for this message. I was grateful God helped me see the truth about His heart. Two disciples show us how listening to conviction versus condemnation leads to very different ends. Read Matthew 26: 69-75, John 21: 15-19 and Acts 4: 1-4, 13. After he denied knowing Jesus, how did Peter later respond to Jesus? What was the result in Peter's life? Did Peter listen to the voice of conviction or condemnation?

> *My sheep recognize my voice. I know them, and they follow me. I give them real and eternal life. They are protected from the Destroyer for good. No one can steal them from out of my hand. The Father who put them under my care is so much greater than the Destroyer and Thief. No one could ever get them away from him. I and the Father are one heart and mind.*
>
> *John 10:27-30,*
> *The Message*

3. Now read Matthew 26: 14-16, Matthew 26: 23-25, Matthew 26: 47-50 and Matthew 27: 3-5. After he betrayed Jesus, what was the end result for Judas? Would Jesus have forgiven Judas had he asked? Whose voice was Judas listening to? Describe that voice.

4. Satan's voice offers burden, clamoring discouragement, condemnation, defeat, looking backward, slavery and a sense of worthlessness. How much of this do you hear?

Read Philippians 4: 6-9. When in doubt, test the voices you hear against this scripture. God's voice is full of life and peace, truth, grace, hope, gentle redirection and encouragement to grow. His voice directs you toward freedom. Even in your failings, you get a sense of being part of an eternal process for goodness.

Sometimes I wish, when we become Christ followers and God gives us a new heart, that He'd also give us new eyeballs because we rarely see ourselves and God as we truly are. Satan takes advantage of our nearsightedness. He'll whisper that we are guilty as charged, too angry to be helpful, too weak to be useful, too prideful to glorify God, too … inadequate.

God tells us in scripture that we're heirs according to the promise, we're Christ's friend, we're united with Him and one in spirit, we're saints, we're bought with a price, we're complete, and we belong to Him.

\* \* \*

In C.S. Lewis' book "Prince Caspian," a battle is raging. While fighting his evil uncle to win the freedom of Old Narnia, the young Prince Caspian waits for help from the only source of help he knows. The talking beasts have sent for Aslan, the savior-redeemer lion. The prince hopes he will arrive before all is lost.

But the Prince must first endure discouragement and deception from within his own ranks.

A dwarf said to the prince: "Either Aslan is dead or he is not on our side. Or else something stronger than himself keeps him back. And if he did come – how do we know he'd be our friend?"

We hear the same lies about God: "Perhaps God's dead or powerless or He's not on our side."

The Bible tells us the "devil prowls around like a roaring lion, looking for someone to devour."

We would be wise to recognize our enemy and fight back.

> *He who vindicates me is near. Who then will bring charges against me? Let us face each other! Who is my accuser? Let him confront me! It is the Sovereign Lord who helps me. Who is he that will condemn me? They will all wear out like a garment; the moths will eat them up.*
>
> *Isaiah 50:8-9*

**Day Two – Godly Sorrow and Confession**

When each of my children reached toddlerhood, I dove into the parenting books because I wanted to know who took my angel and left me with this defiant alien.

The healthy independence of toddlerhood brings some trying times. When my kids were disobedient, I quickly realized the most damaging thing I could do was burden them with guilt. Guilt would focus them away from the real issue. The best thing I could do was let them experience the consequences of their actions so they could feel sorrowful and learn responsibility.

Likewise, God doesn't bear down on us with guilt, keeping us stuck in self-focused immaturity. He allows us to experience the consequences of our choices so that when we mess up, we feel it. He doesn't distract us from the real issue but teaches us to feel sorry about our sin and to take responsibility for our behavior.

Henry Cloud and John Townsend helped me understand the problem with guilt in their book, "How People Grow." They write that because Jesus has already dealt with our guilt, "the Bible says we should not feel guilty, but we should feel sorry. There is a big difference."

Feeling guilty keeps us stuck, focused on ourselves, and unmoved by the damage we've done. In essence, guilt robs us of our capacity to care about those we hurt or the destruction we cause.

Feeling sorrow transforms our heart and develops our sensitivity toward others and God.

> *Now I'm glad – not that you were upset, but that you were jarred into turning things around. You let the distress bring you to God, not drive you from him. The result was all gain, no loss.*
>
> *Distress that drives us to God does that. It turns us around. It gets us back in the way of salvation. We never regret that kind of pain. But those who let distress drive them away from God are full of regrets, end up on a deathbed of regrets.*
>
> *And now, isn't it wonderful all the ways in which this distress has goaded you closer to God? You're more alive, more concerned, more sensitive, more reverent, more human, more passionate, more responsible. Looked at from any angle, you've come out of this with purity of heart.*
>
> 2 Corinthians 7: 9-11,
> The Message

1. Being fully loved and fully known is the best remedy for guilt. Godly sorrow and confession help us experience that remedy. Read 2 Corinthians 7:9-10. What are the differences between godly sorrow and worldly sorrow?

2. Which do you experience most, godly sorrow or worldly sorrow?

3. One of my heroes of the Bible is King David. It comforts me to know the depth of David's sin and how he was still called a man after God's own heart. (You can read David's story in 2 Samuel 11.) Read David's prayer in Psalm 51:1-5. How did David feel before he confessed his sin? When have you felt this way?

4. David knew God desired something from him. What was it? Read Psalm 51:6. Do you ever hedge with God, not quite telling the whole truth? Or are you able to be completely honest?

5. Who can you open up to about your sin and guilt?

## Day Three - Conclusions

1. Although we sin, God doesn't condemn us. My pastor says, "The Only One who can condemn us, doesn't." That's grace. Read the story of the woman caught in the act of adultery in John 8:1-11. How would you have felt if you were the woman in this story?

> *If you're feeling guilty for the things you've done, Jesus forgives you, accepts you, and has a plan for you to do good things. Feeling godly sorrow about your sin will involve you in His plan. Believing that God points an accusing finger at you will keep you stuck.*

2. We sin but God isn't interested in accusing us.

> *This is how much God loved the world: He gave his Son, his one and only Son. And this is why: so that no one need be destroyed; by believing in him, anyone can have a whole and lasting life. God didn't go to all the trouble of sending his Son merely to point an accusing finger, telling the world how bad it was. He came to help, put the world right again. Anyone who trusts in Him is acquitted; anyone who refuses to trust him has long since been under the death sentence without knowing it.*
> *John 3:16-18, The Message*

Read Romans 8:1. As a result of reading this chapter, what conclusions can you draw about guilt and its influence on your life specifically?

Our sin doesn't surprise God. It needn't surprise us. If you struggle with guilt, Jesus wants you to know He has the same unconditional love for you as He had for the woman at the well that hot day in Samaria. He's offering a drink of the living water that alone can satisfy.

> *The Christian faith is the story of God's love for us and our response of love for Him. Whatever goodness is in us is a by-product of our love for Him, not the goal.*

> *Jesus,*
> *At times I feel so guilty I think I might drown. Help me know you that you forgive me, you accept me and you give me good things to do for you and others. Help me learn to feel sorrow instead of guilt. Thank you for paying the price for my sin. Thank you for knowing everything I've ever done and for loving me passionately. I confess these things to you now. I won't shove them under the carpet. Help me turn from them and embrace you. Give me strength to find help from others and learn they can accept me too. Help me ask forgiveness of anyone I've wronged. Keep knowing me and loving me. You are my precious savior.*
> *Amen*

**Group Discussion –** *What can we do about our guilt? What has God done about our guilt?*

**Chapter 5 – Part 1**

1. What spoke loudest to you this week?

2. Do you struggle with people-pleasing guilt? If so, how? What's wrong with people- pleasing guilt?

3. What has God done about sin and guilt, for all of us and for you individually? Read these one at a time and discuss them: Romans 5:8, Romans 8:1, 2 Corinthians 7:9-10 and 2 Corinthians 9:6-7.

4. Are you realizing anything new about guilt?

**Chapter 5 – Part 2**

1. What helped you with your guilt this week?

2. Read 2 Corinthians 7:9-11. What's the difference between guilt and godly sorrow? Which do you lean toward?

3. How might confession help you? What do you need from others when you feel guilty?

4. What is God saying to you about guilt? What crossing do you need to make regarding your guilt?

# Chapter 6
## Shame – Alienation That Breaks the Heart

*Those who look to him are radiant; their faces
are never covered with shame. Psalm 34:5*

*We ask ourselves, 'Who am I to be brilliant,
gorgeous, talented and fabulous?' Actually, who
are you not to be? You are a child of God.*
*Nelson Mandela*

Whenever she crested the last hill on her way home from school, she'd look to see if her father's car was parked in front of the house. If it was, she'd carefully plan how to avoid him. She went directly into her room or to a friend's house. By steering clear of him, she tried to avoid the shame she felt in his presence.

But shame followed her. Although she'd done nothing wrong, she felt as though everyone could see right through her to the loser she knew herself to be.

As a child, she distanced herself from people who could help her. She was afraid to approach her teachers or ask questions in class. As an adult, she felt incapable of performing the simplest jobs, and so she sought employment that required little of her. She wanted to be close to others, but her feelings of being too needy kept her from pursuing relationships. She needed to grow into adulthood before she could understand the power of shame and how it broke her heart.

This is my story of shame.

\*\*\*

The end of Genesis 2 tells us Adam and Eve were "naked, and they felt no shame." What incredible peace – no worries about what to wear!

Then came the forbidden fruit. And early in chapter 3, Adam and Eve are scurrying around sewing up fig leaves for coverage because their eyes were "opened, and they realized they were naked …" Somewhere between the end of chapter 2 and the beginning of chapter 3, shame entered the world.

We paid a big price for Adam and Eve's rebellion. It cost us our connection to our Heavenly Father, an attachment that told us we were precious to Him. Even though God never abandoned us, we felt the wall of our sin come between us. Our disconnection from Him left us with a sense of alienation resulting in shame. Just the way children who aren't vitally connected to their parents feel shame, our severed relationship with our Heavenly Father leaves us with shame.

Shame is another complex subject. There are a variety of definitions, but the key ingredients are alienation from God and others, leaving you with feelings of inadequacy, inferiority, a sense of being bad, and a desire to hide your inner self.

Unlike guilt, you don't have to do anything wrong to feel shame. You feel shame more in who you are than in what you've done. Some describe hearing an inner, critical voice whispering: "You don't measure up. You just can't do anything right."

Shame begins with alienation from God, but if parents or significant others disconnect from us as children, it reinforces feelings of inadequacy. In their book "Letting Go of Shame," Ronald and Patricia Efron write "… parents (can) do their duty but never convey the idea that they treasure their children. Children shamed in this fashion may grow up believing they could never be deeply loved by another human being."

Harsh or critical parenting also brings about shame. You hear shame in the phrases, "Don't cry. Only babies cry," or "Why don't you think before you do things?" or "Keep it to yourself." You see shame in lowered gazes and fidgeting hands.

But whatever our experience, we've all felt shame at one time or another, especially when taking risks with others – on the job, in school, with friends. The effects of shame are often devastating, leading to unmet potential, unfulfilled dreams, depression, rage and even suicide. The insidious nature of shame is that it feels inescapable. After all, the voice of shame says, "You can't escape who you truly are."

There's a woman in the gospels who's a hero of mine. She went to Jesus with her shame and came away knowing she belonged.

***

A crowd gathered around Jesus once again. A prominent religious leader had asked Jesus to heal his dying daughter and the people hustled Him along, hoping to catch a glimpse of the miracle worker in action.

A quietly desperate woman followed him on the fringes of the crowd. She'd been hemorrhaging for 12 long years. The numerous doctors she'd been to took her money but only caused her additional suffering.

Perhaps the most painful of all her problems, however, was being shunned by others. Because of her condition, Jewish law required those who came near her to go through a lengthy cleansing ritual. She was considered unclean. She knew this. She understood it as well as any leper, and shame filled her heart. She learned to hide and obligingly keep her distance.

She'd heard of the miracles Jesus had done. "What if this is the Son of God we've been waiting for?" she thought. "If He has so much power, touching the hem of his robe might be enough to cure me." Moving in to touch Him was risky. Someone might notice. But it was worth a try.

Skillfully she blended into the crowd. Reaching Him was difficult. But she caught hold of Jesus' robe for a moment and, in that moment, she knew she was healed. Stunned, she stood still. And Jesus stopped.

The scripture says that when she touched His robe, Jesus realized power went out of Him. Amazing! Why would God notice power leaving Him? He's God! He created the heavens and the earth. This amount of power was nothing. What purpose did it serve for Him to notice?

But Jesus never wanted to breeze through His life on earth untouched by humanity. He wanted to engage with people. He wanted this woman to know Him. So, He noticed.

He began looking for her. His friends thought He was crazy to try to find one person who had touched Him from among the throng gathered around Him. The people urged Him on. He had more important business to attend to, they said.

But Jesus waited and looked. He knew His work. He was about His Father's business and, at that moment, His Father was caring for a lonely, shame-filled woman who nonetheless had enough faith to take a great risk. Jesus knew she sought physical healing, but He wanted to tell her about a deeper healing. He wanted to set her free not only from her physical pain but from her shame as well. He wanted to tell her who she really was.

She had to force herself to come out of hiding. She had no other option. She'd been found out. Trembling, the outcast woman fell on her knees, and as she wept she blurted out her story.

Then Jesus surprised her. She expected public ridicule and critical words. But He had no desire to shake His finger at her. He took her hand, stood her up in the center of the crowd and, with all eyes fixed on them, He said, "Daughter, your faith has healed you. Go in peace and be freed from your suffering."

What tremendous relief and freedom she must have felt! I'll bet she told everyone she met that the Son of the Living God healed her and called her His Daughter.

She'd learned to hide from others, and yet Jesus sought her out and looked into her eyes. She'd felt only the shame of being an unwanted, problematic woman, but Jesus called her "daughter" and made her His own.

\*\*\*

We're familiar with shame too. We wear it on our heart like a secret badge while Satan whispers that we should be ashamed of ourselves and hide. But no matter what we hide behind, no matter what's been done to us, no matter who others say we are, God sees us and He calls us His own.

From the start of my journey with Him, I felt uncomfortable thinking of God as someone who is relationally intimate. Something kept me at a distance, as though closeness was too casual.

Still, scripture told me that Jesus referred to God as Abba Father, an expression of an especially close relationship. "Abba Father" can be translated as "Daddy." Jesus' use of the name Abba startled the Jews then, and I was startled too. Calling him Abba Father seemed too familiar.

> *For you did not receive a spirit that makes you a slave again to fear, but you received the Spirit of sonship. And by him we cry, 'Abba, Father.' The Spirit himself testifies with our spirit that we are God's children.*
>
> *Romans 8:15-16*

But life brought me to the point where I needed my God to fill in some gaps as a close Father and a loving Daddy. When I felt shame, I needed Him to call me daughter. I needed His nurture and protection and to know He was with me in my anger and grief as well as in my little triumphs and joys. I needed Him to laugh with me.

One night, I poured out to God the shame in my heart and told Him how I longed for Him as Daddy. I heard an immediate response. "Don't you know how I long to *be* your Daddy?"

Those words echoed through my soul as I sat in the stillness of my room. Not only do I have a need for a Daddy, but my Heavenly Father longs to *be* my Daddy.

Incredible!

Like a trusting young child with a passionately devoted Father, that's how intimately the God of the universe wants to know us. His love pulls us out of the mire of earthly shame, for we are precious to the One who made the heavens and the earth. He offers us his peace, and he brings our suffering to an end.

He longs to be my Daddy and yours. That thought still takes my breath away.

*Daughter, your faith has healed you. Go in peace and be freed from your suffering.*
*Mark 5:34*

# Write Your Story

The questions in this section might bring up a lot of pain. Be good to yourself and take it slowly. Don't force anything. Consider taking a walk with God. Ask Him to lead you through these questions and listen for what He might say. Call a trusted friend and ask them to listen to you for a while.

Some of the questions here focus on our relationships with parents, caregivers and others. We need to go back to the root of shame in order to understand where it began and dig it out. And so, we go back to those relationships. Through it all, we need to accept responsibility for our actions and our feelings. This is not a blame session, it's a search for understanding, healing, forgiveness and wholeness.

I encourage you to address your pain as much as you can. Try not to deny it or silence it. Attend to it. God can heal us when we just let the pain be. We keep Him at bay when we run from our broken heart through busyness or laughter. Just as the woman who touched Jesus' robe let her desperation give her courage, you too can be emboldened by your heartache. And Jesus will meet you there.

## Chapter Six – Part One
## Day One – The Heartache of Shame

1. Shame in any form distances us from others. We've all been shamed at one time or another, directly or indirectly. Describe a time when you were rejected or shamed because you didn't measure up in some area. Maybe you've been shamed for:
    - your personality being too boring or too brash, too lazy or too busy.
    - failing athletically – and you got the message you let the whole team down.
    - offering nothing of value – everyone's looking at you for something but is disappointed in what you offer.
    - your feelings and responses. Perhaps you've been shamed for feeling something was wrong in a relationship and talking about it.
    - having a disability.
    - your appearance.

> *The Lord is close to the brokenhearted and saves those who are crushed in spirit.*
>
> *Psalm 34:18*

2. Abuse alienates you from others, making it hard to trust. Have you felt shame for what's been done to you? For example:
    - Have you suffered some type of sexual abuse?
    - Were you told foul jokes, or shown adult movies and pornography by an adult when you were a child?
    - Were you battered?
    - Were you emotionally abused?

3. As children, we feel unworthy of love and incompetent in our work when our parents or other significant adults fail to engage with us emotionally. How did the significant people in your life engage with you when you were young? Did they listen to your feelings and accept them? How did they handle your anger? Did you get the message you were treasured?

4. Read Hebrews 12:2. Jesus is familiar with shame. What did He endure? (Perhaps also read John 18 and 19)

> *There are no ordinary people. You have never talked to a mere mortal. Nations, cultures, arts, civilizations – these are mortal, and their life is to ours as the life of a gnat. But it is immortals whom we joke with, work with, marry, snub, and exploit – immortal horrors or everlasting splendors.*
>
> "The Weight of Glory,"
> *C.S. Lewis*

*Jesus lived, died and lives again to win you back. That's how much your heart means to Him.*

**Day Two – The God Who Sees**

1. Which part of yourself do you feel you must hide from others? You feelings, needs, mistakes? Your appearance? Your intelligence? When did you first begin hiding that part of yourself? Who shamed that part of you?

> *But you are a shield around me, O Lord; you bestow glory on me and lift up my head.*
>
> *Psalm 3:3*

2. What do you hide behind – busyness, laughter, caution, perfection, superiority, having it all together? Or something else?

3. Read the story of Hagar in Genesis 16. What happened to Hagar? What did Hagar call God in Genesis 16:13? How do you feel about the God who sees you and all you've been through?

4. Read Psalm 139:1-16. Summarize this passage in a few sentences and personalize it. What does this mean to you?

> *The Lord your God is with you, he is mighty to save. He will take great delight in you, he will quiet you with his love, he will rejoice over you with singing.*
>
> *Zephaniah 3:17*

## Chapter 6 – Part 2
### Day One – No Longer An Outsider

Shame tells us our God is distant and only engages with those who measure up. But God says we belong to Him.

1. The moment Adam and Eve ate the forbidden fruit, all humanity went from belonging to God to being alienated from Him. It's as though we never knew Him. Read John 1:10. What does this verse mean?

2. We weren't meant for shame and alienation. We were meant to be treasured in our relationships with God and His children. So when sin severed us from God and flooded us with shame, God had a plan to reunite us. Read Ephesians 2:14-19. What did Jesus do about our alienation from God?

3. "It's urgent that you listen carefully to this: Anyone here who believes what I'm saying right now and aligns himself with the Father, who has in fact put me in charge, has at this very moment the real, lasting life and is *no longer condemned to be an outsider*. This person has taken a giant step from the world of the dead to the world of the living." (John 5:24, The Message) Do you feel like you belong or like an outsider to God? What makes you feel that way?

> *Behold I have inscribed you on the palms (of my hands.)*
>
> *Isaiah 49:16a, New American Standard Bible*

4. Read Ephesians 2:19. What would you need from others and God to develop a sense of belonging? Can you ask them for that?

## Day Two – The Great Deception

"In those days, far south in Calormen on a little creek of the sea, there lived a poor fisherman called Arsheesh, and with him there lived a boy who called him Father." So begins C.S. Lewis' story "The Horse and His Boy."

The boy, Shasta, was born a prince. But he was kidnapped as a baby and, as he grew, he was led to believe he was the poor son of a cruel fisherman. It wasn't until he met his real father and twin brother that he realized who he truly was.

You, too, have been deceived. Your enemy, Satan, wants to keep it from you but you belong to your Heavenly Daddy. You are a child of the King.

1. The crowd rejected her as a nuisance, but Jesus called her by her real name. In the story from Mark 5:21-34, Jesus called the sick woman Daughter and changed how she thought of herself. She belonged to someone important. She was the Daughter of the God Most High. What has the voice of shame called you? What has the God Most High called you?

> *It seems odd to have to say so, but too much religion is a bad thing. We can't get too much of God, can't get too much faith and obedience, can't get too much love and worship. But religion – the well-intentioned efforts we make to "get it all together" for God – can very well get in the way of what God is doing for us. The main and central action is everywhere and always what God has done, is doing, and will do for us.*
>
> The Message
> *Eugene H. Peterson*

2. Our earthly father and mother color our view of God. If you were neglected or treated harshly by your parents, thinking of God as Daddy might be hard for you. Read Exodus 34:6 where God describes Himself. Then, ask Him to help you differentiate between your earthly father and your Heavenly Father. Developing relationships with spiritual fathers and mothers in God's family of believers can help. Be gentle with yourself. It takes time to develop confidence that God can be trusted with the most tender part of your heart. Write a prayer asking God to heal you and show you what a loving father truly can be.

## Day Three – When I am Weak, Then I Am Strong

We think we have to stay on top of our game to avoid feeling shame and revealing weakness. But the Bible tells us something different.

1. Read 2 Corinthians 12:8-10. What does the author do with his weaknesses? How does he view them? What does your weakness drive you to do?

2. God is always at work for good. All your weakness, if it causes you to lean on God and others, is being used for good. What goodness might God want to bring you from your weakness?

3. It was weakness, not strength, that drove the sick woman to reach out for Jesus' robe. Have you reached out to touch the hem of His robe? Have you ever been so desperate to be free of shame that you were willing to risk everything? What brought you to the point of desperation and what happened when you got there?

> *For though we live in the world, we do not wage war as the world does. The weapons we fight with are not the weapons of the world. On the contrary, they have divine power to demolish strongholds. We demolish arguments and every pretension that sets itself up against the knowledge of God, and we take captive every thought to make it obedient to Christ.*
>
> *2 Corinthians 10:3-5*

4. God wants us to engage with each other. (Romans 12:15, Romans 15:7, Galatians 5:13) And He uses others to set us free from shame. To that end, it's very helpful to talk openly with safe people. Get to know people before diving in deep, however, because not everyone is ready to hear brokenness … and they might add to yours. But there are those who will listen without judging. And there are helpful counselors. (Talk to your discussion leader or call your local church about recommended counselors in your area.) Have you confided in anyone about your shame? What is your greatest fear about revealing your shame? What do you think might happen if you opened up to trustworthy people about your shame?

My crossing from shame to belonging began by first attending to my heart. I acknowledged the shame to myself and Jesus and then to others by talking with a gentle counselor and trustworthy friends. It was frightening to admit my shame to others. I was afraid they'd shame me, too. But they loved me, and I'm eternally grateful. They helped me see the lies I believed about myself and told me that many others felt the way I did. Their words and care were transforming.

After I started believing their words, I realized my view of myself differed from scripture's perspective. I needed to stop believing the lies. It wasn't that I refused to believe God, it's just that I really thought His voice was the one I heard shaming me. So, I found scriptures that countered every shameful voice I'd ever heard. I wrote them down on cards and carried them around with me. Every time I heard a shameful voice, I pulled out those scriptures and tested the shaming voice against God's voice. If the two didn't match – and they never did – I tossed out the voice of shame and believed God's truth. I took captive every thought to make it obedient to Christ. (2 Corinthians 10:5)

It was a long, hard road to change my beliefs about myself, but that process still profoundly impacts me today. Here are some of those scriptures.
- Romans 8:1
- Jeremiah 31:3-4
- Zephaniah 3:17
- Psalm 23
- Psalm 73:26
- Psalm 45:11
- Psalm 25:1-3
- 1 Corinthians 6:19-20

We need to experience scripture to be healed by it, so God uses others to bring scripture to life. When someone else can hear your shame and not condemn you but accept you, scripture will live in your heart and you will have found a treasure.

> *Dear Jesus,*
>
> *You are compassionate, honest and gracious. You are full of gentleness and justice, holiness and humility. Kindness, love and goodness flow from you.*
>
> *I want to look more like you and to believe I already resemble you because you made me. Help me to see myself the way you see me. Help me to know I belong to you, the God Most High. I need to belong to others. Help me with that. Help me trade shame and alienation for belonging to you and your children.*
>
> *I need you.*
> *Amen*

**Group Discussion** – *What can we do about our shame? What has God done about it?*

**Chapter Six – Part One**
1. What stood out to you from the chapter this week?

2. What kind of shame weighs heaviest on your heart these days?

3. Read Psalm 139:1-16. What does this passage mean to you?

4. What is God's view of you in your area of shame?

**Chapter Six – Part Two**
1. What helped you with your shame this week?

2. Read about the woman who brought her shame to Jesus in Mark 5:21-34. Have you been able to bring your shame to Jesus?

3. What has the voice of shame called you? What has the voice of the Most High God called you?

4. How can others help you with your shame? What do you need from others when you feel shame?

5. What crossing is He prompting you to make regarding your shame?

# Chapter 7
# Fear – Losing Sight of His Presence

*Be strong and courageous. Do not be terrified;
do not be discouraged, for the Lord your God will be
with you wherever you go.*

*Joshua 1:9b*

When my son Garrett was younger, he had some frightening nightmares – the kind you don't just snap out of. One night, he woke up and called out to us. Groggy as could be, I rolled out of bed and went to his room. I held him and tried to convince him there were no monsters in the closet and that he was perfectly safe. After a while he seemed to calm down, and I told him I needed to go back to my bed. But he didn't want me to leave him alone.

It wasn't enough for me to come to his bedside, comfort him and go. He wasn't convinced all was safe. And so, eventually, we headed up to my room where he camped out on the floor next to my husband and me until morning.

This kind of late-night routine happened numerous times during his tender years. Through those nights, Garrett taught me there was one thing that would comfort him – our presence.

We need that same kind of comfort because, like my youngest son, we can't always be convinced there really aren't monsters in the closet.

Fear shatters the heart and freezes the limbs. That's to be expected, because we weren't made to live with so many unknowns and so many dangers. We were made to trust in a big God.

There's a huge list of things that scare us. Fear keeps us from speaking in front of groups, from job interviews and displays of talent. It keeps us from committing to established relationships and from developing new ones. Fear keeps us from flying on planes and driving in cars. Reminders of past trauma can trigger present fears. The list goes on and on. You know what I'm talking about – you have your own list.

When we're afraid and we can't be convinced all is safe, God offers us himself, his presence. He says, "Don't be afraid for I'm with you." Like a loving father, He's saying, "I've got you. I'll hold you when the water gets too deep."

> *Where can I go from your Spirit? Where can I flee from your presence? ... If I rise on the wings of the dawn, if I settle on the far side of the sea, even there your hand will guide me, your right hand will hold me fast*
>
> *Psalm 139: 7,9*

\*\*\*

After a long day of healing the sick and teaching the people, Jesus told Peter and his buddies to go on ahead to the other side of the lake.

They got into their boat, and at first all was calm as they sailed to their destination. But about three miles out, the wind suddenly whipped up, the waves grew large and their small boat shook in the water. They tried to bail the water out faster than it was coming in, but things looked bad. As water poured into the boat, they anxiously tried to stay afloat. Then looking through the waves, they saw something … or someone … on the water. In the darkness and splashing, they thought they saw a ghost. Understandably, they were terrified.

But what looked like a ghost turned out to be Jesus walking on the water. Calling out to them he said, "Don't be scared. It's me. I'm here. I've got you."

Now, some people might be comforted by these words. Me? Not so much. If I'm on a small boat in a big lake with the wind and waves whipping at my face, I need more than a few words to find courage.

Most of the disciples felt like I would have. They didn't budge. They were staying put in the comfort of that tiny, rocking, out-of-control boat.

But Peter found confidence in Jesus' words, and he was confident in himself. He wanted to be with Jesus, and he seemed to temporarily forget how big the waves were, how wet the water was. He asked permission to go to Jesus, and then he got *out* of the boat.

In the church today, we like giving Peter a hard time. He's impetuous. He doesn't exactly conduct market research before diving in. But notice, Peter was the only one to get out of the boat. Everyone else was intimidated by those waves. Peter was so focused on getting to Jesus that He, too, walked on water for a moment.

What a great moment that must have been – to feel the water like solid ground beneath your feet and to see Jesus standing there smiling, arms open, waiting for you to come over, like a father at his child's first swimming lesson.

But the miraculous moment didn't last. Peter "saw the wind," or at least the impact of it. The more he stared at the powerful waves and felt the lashing of the wind, the less he looked at Jesus. And the bigger the waves grew, the smaller Jesus was. I suspect it dawned on Peter that he shouldn't be able to walk on water at all.

He forgot that it wasn't his own power that had brought him this far – it was Jesus' power. And probably, like all of us would, he forgot what he'd seen Jesus do – that Jesus had just fed 5,000 people with a few loaves of bread and a couple fish and here He was walking on the water.

Peter started to sink, but before going under he called out for help: "Lord, save me!"

He didn't have to wait long. Immediately, Jesus offered Peter His hand, raised him out of the thrashing water and held up his trembling body. And on their way back to the boat, Jesus reminded Peter that even though his faith would fail him, God would never fail him.

Like a gentle father, God offers us His hand, too. He's not surprised by our fear and He won't shame us for it. He has a big, strong hand, and He wants us to put our little hand in it. Jesus says "Don't be afraid. I'm here. I've got you."

*** 

Notice what Jesus didn't do. First, He didn't tell Peter to remain in the boat where he was safe. He didn't criticize Peter's walking-on-water abilities. After he

> *Let us fix our eyes on Jesus, the author and perfecter of our faith, who for the joy set before him endured the cross, scorning its shame, and sat down at the right hand of the throne of God.*
>
> Hebrews 12:2

started to sink, Jesus didn't remind him that he'd had enough swimming lessons to make it back to the boat on his own. And He didn't recite a dozen scriptures about why Peter *shouldn't* be afraid. In short, Jesus didn't judge Peter and reject him because he was afraid. No, the scripture says, "Immediately, Jesus reached out His hand and caught him."

Jesus doesn't criticize us or disapprove of us when we're afraid. He reaches out His hand to us. That's important to us because, of all our fears, our fear of rejection and abandonment is among the greatest.

Fear of rejection forms the underpinning of many other fears, and it drives many of our unhealthy choices and behaviors. We are, after all, relational creatures. We long for connection and love. Being rejected or experiencing disapproval is extremely hard to take. So Jesus offers us His hand, His presence. And in His presence He offers acceptance and love.

Sometimes when we're afraid, though, even God's presence feels intimidating and we'll have struggles to work through with Him. When our oldest child, Lauren, was almost a year old, I was delightfully surprised to find I was pregnant with our second child. But shortly after Karl and I began joyfully planning to embrace our new little one, I developed symptoms of a pending miscarriage.

You'd think prayer would have been my automatic response. But talking to God was difficult for me. Once, while my doctor ran a series of diagnostic tests, I waited alone in a cold hospital room, unable to even pray. I was too afraid to talk to the God who could save my baby but might not choose to do so. I was too afraid of answers I might get and didn't want.

*And then what?*

The wind and waves loomed large in my mind. I felt a bitter loneliness – knowing He was there, knowing He loved me, but afraid to acknowledge His presence, afraid of what might happen.

In the end, we lost our baby. It was one of the saddest seasons of my life.

But one thing sustained me – the promise God gives us. No matter what happens, no matter how afraid I am, no matter how I feel toward Him, God will still be God. He will offer His hand and hold me through all the frightening storms of my life. Although my faith will fail, His power and presence never will. He says, "I'm here. I've got you."

> *If we don't know how or what to pray, it doesn't matter. He does our praying in and for us, making prayer out of our wordless sighs, our aching groans. He knows us far better than we know ourselves… and keeps us present before God.*
>
> *Romans 8:26-27,*
> The Message

And, just like my frightened son years ago, when I can't be convinced all is safe, I am always invited to camp out on His floor.

> *...for the Lord will go before you,*
> *The God of Israel will be your rear guard.*
> *Isaiah 52:12b*

# Write Your Story

Sometimes I have to catch myself. When pain comes, I realize that one of the things I look to God for is a rescue from the heartache of this world. "God, I thought if I … then you would …" I want someone to swoop me into his arms and save me. But God didn't promise safety. He promised His goodness to a world full of pain.

We struggle to understand why we suffer under a good God. If God is good, our logic goes, why do these horrible things happen? And these questions are at the root of some of our greatest fears. C.S. Lewis addresses the concept of God's goodness in his book, "The Lion, The Witch and the Wardrobe."

In the book, four children enter the magical land of Narnia. It's complete with a White Witch, talking animals and Aslan the Lion, who represents Christ.

In one of my favorite parts of the story, the four children don't yet know who Aslan is and they must rely on their new friends, the Beavers, to tell them.

> "Is – is he a man?" asked Lucy.
>
> "Aslan, a man!" said Mr. Beaver sternly. "Certainly not. I tell you he is the King of the wood and the son of the great Emperor-Beyond-the Sea. Don't you know who is the King of Beasts? Aslan is a lion – the Lion, the great Lion."
>
> "Ooh!" said Susan, "I'd thought he was a man. Is he – quite safe? I shall feel rather nervous about meeting a lion."
>
> "That you will, dearie, and no mistake," said Mrs. Beaver, "if there's anyone who can appear before Aslan without their knees knocking, they're either braver than most or else just silly."
>
> "Then he isn't safe?" said Lucy.
>
> "Safe?" said Mr. Beaver. "Don't you hear what Mrs. Beaver tells you? Who said anything about safe? 'Course he isn't safe. But he's good. He's the King, I tell you."

> *We live in a world of God's permissive will, not His perfect will. Life as we know it here is God's second choice, or maybe even his $10^{th}$ or $20^{th}$ or $1,000^{th}$.*

Like Aslan, God can always be counted on for goodness – but we shouldn't expect him to behave as we'd like. John Eldredge calls this the "wildness of God."

## Day One – He's Good But He's Not Tame

1. How do you respond to the statement: "God is good, but He's not safe, tame or predictable?"

2. You aren't alone if you feel unsteadied by God's unpredictability. Sometimes God is silent, and sometimes he seems far off just when we need Him. Read Psalm 10:1 and Psalm 22:1-2. What feelings does the Psalmist express? Can you relate to the writers of these Psalms? Do you feel afraid or abandoned by God's lack of predictability?

3. Through all that happens to us on this planet, God is always at work for goodness and redemption. While we're alive, terrible things can happen to us, and sometimes we're unable to see a redemptive thread in the circumstances of our lives. But God sees all things and loves us. He can be counted on for goodness.

    One man in the Old Testament experienced more suffering than most of us will ever know. But somehow, through all his heartache, Job continued to believe in God's plan to bring goodness out of evil. Read what Job said about God in Job 19:25. When something is "redeemed," it's bought back by the owner. List the troubles you've been through and look for a thread of redemption running through them. What is that thread? What goodness might God want to bring from your heartache?

4. Write a prayer expressing any fear you have of God as the great untamed lion. Thank Him for anything you find that's good. If you found a thread of redemption, talk with Him about it and praise Him for it. If you couldn't find a thread of redemption, ask Him to show you one.

> *So much pain and no good reason why.*
> *You've cried until the tears run dry.*
> *And nothing here can make you understand.*
> *The one thing that you held so dear is slipping from your hands.*
> *And you say, 'Why, why, why does it go this way?*
> *Why, why, why' and all I can say is*
> *Somewhere down the road there'll be answers to the questions.*
> *Somewhere down the road though we cannot see it now.*
> *Somewhere down the road you will find mighty arms reaching for you.*
> *And they will hold the answers at the end of the road.*
> *"Somewhere Down the Road,"*
> *Amy Grant and Wayne Kirkpatrick*

**Day Two – We're all afraid**
1. Read Numbers 13:1-3, 21-14:25. This is the story of Israel at the edge of the Promised Land, the land they had generations to claim. What kept them from making the crossing into the Promised Land?

2. Read Numbers 13:32-33. Do you ever feel like a grasshopper, tiny and powerless? What makes you afraid?
    - trusting others
    - confronting others' intimidating ways
    - going new places
    - job interviews
    - pursuing a dream
    - enduring an illness
    - losing loved ones
    - financial burdens
    - fill in the blank

3. Your fear is grounded in something. In this dangerous world, God uses fear to warn us … because sometimes there really are monsters in the closet. Often, though, we're afraid to let go of the very things that hurt us. Your fear could be grounded in events from earlier in your life. If you were in a bad car accident, a fender bender can trigger a fear-based reaction. If you were abused, seeing someone who reminds you of the abuser will trigger fear. Are you aware of earlier traumatic events in your life that can trigger fear in you today?

4. Fear is good and bad. When we were young, we were taught to stay away from the hot stove so we wouldn't get burned. Sometimes God's blessing comes in the form of fear as an early warning system. If you repeatedly put yourself in harmful situations or relationships, your fear is a gift from God. All the prayer and Bible study in the world won't help, because you're afraid for a good reason. You could take that gift of fear and use it to make a move. Are you holding on to the very thing that's hurting you?

5. Read Romans 12: 9-10. When patterns run deep, we find ourselves repeating the pain of our past and we cling to what we know rather than risk the unknown. Are there unhealthy patterns, habits or people you're clinging to and afraid to leave? Is there a crossing you need to make regarding fear?

### Day Three – Living With Fear Costs Us Our Vision

1. When we're afraid, we get very short-sighted. We lose sight of His presence and His actions on our behalf. But there's more going on than meets the eye. Read 2 Kings 6:8-17. What was Elisha's servant afraid of?

> *So we're not giving up. How could we! Even though on the outside it often looks like things are falling apart on us, on the inside, where God is making new life, not a day goes by without his unfolding grace. These hard times are small potatoes compared to the coming good times, the lavish celebration prepared for us. There's far more here than meets the eye. The things we see now are here today, gone tomorrow. But the things we can't see now will last forever.*
>
> *2 Corinthians 4: 16-18.*

2. What did Elisha believe would help his servant? And what happened?

3. What do your eyes need to see? Spiritually and practically speaking, how can you open your eyes?

**Day Four – When We're Afraid**
1. Read the story of Jesus walking on water in Matthew 14:22-33. How did Peter respond when he started to sink? What other options did he have?

2. What do you do when you feel afraid and you're starting to sink? Does your way of coping with fearful things help move you to where you and God want to go, or is it more of a hindrance?

3. Is God prompting you to push through on anything you're afraid of? Do you sense Jesus calling you to get out of the boat? Describe that.

4. What are you hoping for in the final days of this study?

> *For I am the Lord, your God, who takes hold of your right hand and says to you, Do not fear; I will help you. Don't be afraid ... for I myself will help you, declares the Lord, your Redeemer, the Holy One of Israel.*
>
> *Isaiah 41:13-14*

## Day Five – The Presence Of God and Others

On the morning of Sept. 11, 2001, my neighbor called to tell me about the attacks on the Twin Towers. Through that awful morning, we spoke on the phone several times. Each of us had tasks to accomplish that day, but we needed the comfort of one another's presence.

I've learned that when I'm afraid and fear isolates me, God offers me His presence and the presence of others. He understands my fear and He wants to come alongside me. When God says, "Don't be afraid, because I am with you," He's talking about more than just showing up.

1. Read Genesis 26:24, Numbers 14:9, Psalm 23:4, Isaiah 41:10 and Hebrews 13:5-6. What does scripture mean when it says God is with them? What does His presence give them the courage to do?

2. God has a master plan to restore you and free you from fear of judgment and punishment. Read 1 John 4:15-18. According to this passage, what's included in God's plan to free you from fear?

3. 1 John 4:15-18 can also relate to our fear of rejection by others. How might perfect love drive out our fear of rejection by others?

4. God designed us to depend on one another in relationships. So it seems reasonable that our deepest fears would be rooted in our fear of rejection or abandonment. When have you been rejected? What role does the fear of rejection play in your life today? In other words, what do you find yourself doing to avoid rejection? (Being perfect?)

> *My prayers are nothing other than a sense of the presence of God.*
> "Practicing His Presence,"
> *Brother Lawrence*

5. God's plan of restoration calls for us to lean on trustworthy people to break through the fear of rejection. Read Romans 12:13-16. How are we to relate to one another? What do you want someone to say or do when you're afraid?

6. What's been especially helpful in this chapter that you'd like to remember? Which verse(s) are significant to you that you could memorize and recall when you're afraid?

Like guilt and shame, the thing that makes fear so monstrous in our hearts is keeping it hidden. We're afraid to tell others how afraid we are! But how would you feel if someone came alongside you and listened to your fear and didn't judge you or otherwise minimize your fear?

Frequently, God offers His hand to us through others. That means we need to let others in on our fear. We can ask others to pray for us and with us. And we can just talk about the fear.

Some of my greatest times of growth came from telling others about why and how I was afraid. I've felt crazy for telling them, and I feared they'd agree. But I formed new bonds and decreased my fear just by talking about it with a trustworthy soul.

> *I sought the Lord and he answered me; he delivered me from all my fears.*
> *Psalm 34:4*

> *Jesus,*
> *At times I'm so filled with fear. It makes me want to hide. It makes me want to give up. Please help me overcome my fear. Thank you for being with me through it. I need you so much. Make me courageous. Show me anything I can do to combat the fear. Show me where it comes from when I can't figure that out. Help me even today to see you being with me and helping me along through this fear. I love you.*
> *Amen*

**Discussion Questions –** *What can we do about fear? What has God done about fear?*
1. What do you want to remember from this chapter?

2. What fears are haunting you right now?

3. What do you need from God and others when you're afraid? Be specific.

4. What do you think about the concept that God is good but not safe?

5. Read Psalm 23:4, Isaiah 41:10 and Matthew 14:22-33. How can these scriptures help you with your fear?

6. What are you hoping for as you come to the final chapters?

# Chapter 8
# When God Waits

*When Jesus saw her sobbing and the Jews with her sobbing, a deep anger welled up within him. He said, 'Where did you put him?'*

*'Master, come and see,' they said. Now Jesus wept.*

*John 11:33-35, The Message*

For days, Lazarus lay sick in bed. His sisters frantically scurried around, trying every remedy they knew, but he only grew weaker and more distant. Mary and Martha feared his illness would end in death. But they had one hope: Jesus. He was the only One who could heal Lazarus now.

Jesus was only a day's journey away. Urgently, they sent word. "Lord, the one you love is sick." They needn't say more. They knew Jesus would come. He loved Lazarus and He loved them. He wouldn't let Lazarus die.

But when Jesus heard the news, He waited.

The days wore on and there was no sign of Jesus coming. Lazarus' was fading fast, and Mary and Martha wept at their brother's bedside.

And then, despite their prayers and pleadings, he died. And still Jesus didn't come.

They began to question everything they knew about Jesus. He loves us, they thought, and he has the power to heal. So why? Why did He abandon us when we needed Him most?

Finally, four days after Lazarus died, Jesus arrived. "Too little, too late," some muttered. When Martha heard He was nearby, she went out to meet Him. Faith mingled with doubt as she poured out her disappointment. "Lord, if you had been here, my brother would not have died. But I know that even now God will give you whatever you ask."

Then Jesus said something to Martha that should rock our world. "I am the resurrection and the life. He who believes in me will live even though he dies; and whoever lives and believes in me will never die. Do you believe this?"

He was either crazy or He really was the Son of the Living God. Nobody walks around guaranteeing eternal life in exchange for a following.

But there wasn't time to absorb it all. Mary came and fell at Jesus' feet, weeping. "Lord, if you had been here," she cried, "my brother would not have died." Her friends were with her, and the sounds of grief enveloped Jesus.

When He heard their mourning, the silent wailing of millions of other anguished, broken hearts rang in His ears. Tears from losses of the past, present and future splashed at His feet. He stared at all the death and brokenness sin had created. Anger rose up inside Him, and He wept.

Those watching Jesus wondered why He didn't do anything to prevent Lazarus' death, why he didn't show up four days earlier. After all, He healed the blind man. And, "Look at how He loved Lazarus," they said.

When He came to the tomb, Jesus told those gathered there to remove the stone covering it. (And this part I love, because it reminds us that the Bible is filled with stories about real people.) But the people were reluctant to remove the stone because of the stench. "He's been dead four days and he's sending up quite a stink!" They had no idea what Jesus was about to do.

But Jesus convinced them the stench was beside the point, so they opened up the tomb. And as the cold smell of death blew in their faces, Jesus prayed and called, "Lazarus, come out!"

And He did.

\*\*\*

Like Mary and Martha, sometimes we feel abandoned by the God who loves us. Sometimes, Jesus seems unresponsive to our pleas. We know it's a big, scary world out there, and anything can happen to us. We'd like Him to come when we call.

Ever since sin blew into our world, it's been easier for us to try to dictate to God than to trust Him. But we can't control Jesus' responses. We aren't robots, and neither is He. Jesus works according to His Father's timeline, not ours.

Yet our pain moves Him. And His tears are one of the most profound signs of that.

Jesus wept that day at Lazarus' tomb. He grieved, was deeply moved – "angry," in the original language. But why? Losing a friend could account for some of His pain. Seeing the loss etched in His friends' faces could account for more. But when He came to Lazarus' tomb, Jesus knew He was about to raise His friend from the dead. He and the others there were all about to see Lazarus again. So when He looked at the grief on the faces of His loved ones and wept, He must have been seeing more than just their reaction to Lazarus' death. He must have seen something we can't.

> *For I have come down from heaven not to do my will but to do the will of him who sent me. And this is the will of him who sent me, that I shall lose none of all that he has given me, but raise them up at the last day.*
>
> *John 6:38-39*

Because He's God, Jesus could look across the ages and see how sin had caused the death of all things – the death of relationships, the death of a world once free of pollution and corruption, the death of belief and trust, the death of the heart.

He saw all our suffering that day in Bethany – mothers crying out for their dying children, marriages shipwrecked, children abused, slavery, hatred, lies and abandonment. He mourned not just for the death of Lazarus and the heartbreak of his friends that day – He mourned death and heartbreak for all time.

Jesus wept because death wasn't His plan. Life was His plan.

\*\*\*

Sometimes when we need Him most, God waits. Especially when we're confronted with loss – the loss of someone we love, a marriage, good health, a job –

we feel alone, angry, unable to manage this wild God. But all the while He's suffering with us.

When Whitworth University professor Gerald Sittser was a young husband and a father of four young children, he lost his wife, his mother and one of his daughters in a tragic car accident. He spent the following years learning to care for his grieving children while attending to his own grief. In his book "A Grace Disguised," he writes about the God who suffers with us.

He puts it this way:

> *"The God I know has experienced pain and therefore understands my pain. In Jesus I have felt God's tears, trembled before his death on the cross, and witnessed the redemptive power of his suffering. The Incarnation means that God cares so much that he chose to become human and suffer loss, though he never had to. I have grieved long and hard and intensely. But I have found comfort knowing that the sovereign God, who is in control of everything, is the same God who has experienced the pain I live with every day. No matter how deep the pit into which I descend, I keep finding God there. He is not aloof from my suffering but draws near to me when I suffer. He is vulnerable to pain, quick to shed tears, and acquainted with grief. God is a suffering sovereign who feels the sorrow of the world."*

When writer Phillip Yancey was a baby, his father was stricken with polio, spent several months in the hospital and then died. During his hospital stay, he kept pictures of his family near his bedside; Yancey says he believes his father prayed for him.

But when he was a boy, Yancey was unaware his father had loved him – he'd never known the man. When he was grown, however, his mother told him his father had kept his baby son's pictures at his bedside in his last months. Yancey was deeply loved, but he didn't know it.

Jesus brought Lazarus to life, but he would die again – his return to physical life was only temporary. As devastating as it was for Mary and Martha to wait for Jesus, there was a greater miracle in the making. Jesus' miracle was giving life, everlasting life, to all who believe in Him.

In Jesus, human suffering and God's compassion are met in one heart. When we suffer a loss, we cry out about our anger, abandonment, loneliness and grief. But even if we don't feel it, we can be confident of this – when loss and tragedy strike, God hears us. He weeps with us and He weeps for us.

> *I know that my Redeemer lives, and that in the end he will stand upon the earth.*
>
> *Job 19:25*

# Write Your Story

### Day One – Abandoned by God

1. We don't live long on this earth before we experience loss. What loss have you suffered?
   - Loss of a loved one
   - Loss of a marriage
   - Loss of a job/career
   - Loss of health through illness or injury
   - Loss of emotional stability
   - Loss of a dream
   - Name the loss you've experienced

2. It's hard to imagine anything lonelier than feeling abandoned by God, but it happens to many of us. Read the story of Jesus raising Lazarus in John 11:1-45. There's a great tide if back-and-forth in our human emotions – the pouring out of grief and anger, and the gritty determination to praise God with a broken heart. What were Mary and Martha feeling, and how did they express their feelings to Jesus? And how does Jesus respond to them?

3. Fill in the blank. Jesus, if you had only _____, then _____.

4. Read Psalm 42. Which emotions and thoughts do you see in Mary and Martha that are also in the Psalm?

5. Read Hebrews 4:16. What does the Bible suggest we do in our time of need? What do you want to tell Jesus about your loss at this moment? What do you want to ask Him?

God won't be controlled by us, but He doesn't abandon us either. He's asking us to trust Him like little children who rely completely on their parents, trusting in their goodness.

Many of us have been wounded by parents, and so it's hard to make the leap to trusting a good Heavenly Father. But God isn't our earthly parents, He's God.

### Day Two — Jesus' Tears

His mother, Mary, stood at the foot of the cross while Jesus hung there, dying. She felt every pound of the hammer, every lash of the whip, every last beat of His heart, for she loved Him dearly. He was her son.

When someone I love is hurting, I can almost feel it myself. When we love deeply, we too feel the heartache of those we love deeply.

God didn't create us and then leave us on our own. He embraces our heart with its troubles and joys. When our heart breaks, He weeps. He can give us nothing more precious.

> *Imagine a god who could create people to love and a world for them to live in – knowing in advance the heartache in store for both Him and His people. It's either the craziest scheme ever devised, or the most profound love the universe has ever known.*

1. Notice Jesus' emotions in John 11: 5, 33, 35 and 38. How did Jesus feel about Mary, Martha and Lazarus? And how do you feel as you see Jesus weeping with Mary and Martha?

2. Of all the things others offer me when I'm hurting, understanding, caring and acceptance are the greatest gifts. The tears of others on my behalf touch my soul. And often I experience healing just from knowing someone is with me in this way. Have you noticed this in yourself? Can it be that God has been weeping with you and for you through all your brokenness? Tell Jesus how you feel about His tears on your behalf.

3. Read Isaiah 53:5. When we suffer, we are perhaps closer to God than at any other time. What has His suffering meant to you?

> *"Whenever you find tears in your eyes, especially unexpected tears, it is well to pay the closest attention. They are not only telling you something about the secret of who you are, but more often than not, God is speaking to you through them of the mystery of where you have come from and summoning you to where, if your soul is to be saved, you should go next."*
>
> *Frederick Buechner*

## Day Three – God Waits with Purpose

Like Mary and Martha, at times we'll feel God is far off instead of with us. We have too much to conquer emotionally, mentally, spiritually and physically to feel at home with Him at all times. Whatever the cause, though, the feeling of distance stems from our limitations, not God's. He's present and loving us all along.

1. Read John 11:4-6. Why did Jesus wait?

> *And we, who with unveiled faces all reflect the Lord's glory, are being transformed into his likeness with ever-increasing glory, which comes from the Lord, who is the Spirit.*
>
> *2 Corinthians 3:18*

2. Read John 11:14-15. Why was Jesus glad? Is there anything you sense Jesus is glad about for your sake?

3. Through Lazarus, Jesus displayed His power over death, brought glory to God and caused the people to believe. Read Isaiah 61:1-3. God wants to mend your broken heart and crown you with beauty instead of ashes. You are a planting of the Lord for the display of His splendor. He has a plan to display His power and glory through you. What might that plan include? Ask Him about that plan.

## Day Four – God Wired Us Up To Need Others

In our home we have two pets – a dog and a cat. I like them both, but they're very different.

I've decided dogs are like people and cats are like … cats. Dogs were designed to run in packs. They need each other. They get lonely, bored and into trouble when they're isolated for very long.

Cats are like cats. They don't need anybody. You can't even license a cat because you can't legally own a cat. Cats are completely self-contained, and, if you try to convince them otherwise, you're going to hear about it.

When people disconnect from others, especially when they're hurting, they end up experiencing higher rates of depression, ill health and a whole list of other problems.

We need people because God loves us through them. Sometimes we're wounded by others, and so we think dependence on others is a lousy system. But it's real and necessary. The way to healing after a loss is to pour out our feelings, no matter what they are, to God and others.

1. Mary and Martha needed each other. They went to Jesus for help and they helped each other through the loss of their brother. Read 1 John 3:16-20. List the benefits of being connected in loving relationships. Include in your list what's said about condemnation from our own hearts.

2. When Job was in crisis, his friends tried to help. In many ways they provide a lesson in what not to do for friends in need, but how did they start out? How did they help Job when he was brokenhearted? Read Job 2:11-13.

3. What's the best thing someone has done for you when you suffered a loss? What would you like from others when you're hurting in the future?

> *Give all you know of yourself to all you know of God.*
> *Marvin Webster*

4. Like us, others aren't perfect. They're broken too. Have you ever been on the receiving end of well-meant but hurtful words when you're already suffering? Write about that.

5. Your heart longs for connection with others, and when you suffer, that's an opportunity for others to engage with you deeply. Can you let them in? What could you ask of a friend that would cause you to feel loved today?

**Group Discussion –** *What's happening when God seems silent and far away?*

1. What stood out to you from this chapter?

2. What loss have you suffered?

3. Fill in the blank. Jesus if you had only_____ then_____.

4. When you're hurting and God doesn't seem to show up, what might be going on? Read John 11:1-45.

5. What do you need from others when you suffer loss? What do you need right now?

6. How might God use your brokenness for His glory?

# Chapter 9
## Home – The Promise of God with Us

*The Word became flesh and made his dwelling among us. We have seen his glory, the glory of the One and Only, who came from the Father, full of grace and truth.*

*John 1:14*

In "The Witch of Blackbird Pond," Elizabeth George Speare tells the story of free-spirited Kit Tyler, a young woman living in the 1600s. After her beloved grandfather dies, Kit is forced to leave her beautiful, peaceful home in Barbados and come to the legalistic Puritan colony of Connecticut. At the first sight of her new home, she feels out of place – and her sense of alienation is confirmed again and again by her new neighbors.

But Kit makes a friend in Hannah, an old Quaker woman and town outcast. Hannah helps Kit navigate through this new land. One day, longing for home, Kit runs to Hannah after being humiliated by the town schoolmaster.

"What am I to do now?" she pleaded. "How can I ever go back and face them?"

Hannah said nothing for quite a long time. Her faded eyes studied the girl beside her, and now there was nothing childlike in that wise, kindly gaze.

"Come," she said. "I have something to show thee."

Outside the house, against a sheltered wall to the south, a single stalk of green thrust upward, with slender rapierlike leaves and one huge scarlet blossom. Kit went down on her knees.

"It looks just like the flowers at home," she marveled. "I didn't know you had such flowers here."

"It came all the way from Africa, from the Cape of Good Hope," Hannah told her. "My friend brought the bulb to me, a little brown thing like an onion. I doubted it would grow here, but it just seemed determined to keep on trying and look what has happened."

Kit glanced up suspiciously. Was Hannah trying to preach to her? But the old woman merely poked gently at the earth around the alien plant.

> *I am coming to you now, but I say these things while I am still in the world, so that they may have the full measure of my joy within them. I have given them your word and the world has hated them, for they are not of the world any more than I am of the world.*
>
> *Jesus*, praying for His disciples in *John 17:13-14*

\*\*\*

Hannah was a wise woman. She'd weathered many storms, so she was in a position to help Kit through hers. Hannah was imprisoned in Massachusetts, flogged across the border and eventually had her house burned by neighbors in Connecticut. She was familiar with shame and violence.

Hannah tended her scarlet flower and watched it grow and blossom, although it wasn't planted in its native soil. And she knew Kit – like the flower – could grow and bloom. It would be a struggle, but she could learn to adjust and even thrive in this place so far from her home.

> *Made for heaven. Made, through all the struggle, joy, suffering, and seeming chance of this brief earthly life, for an eternity of bliss no fantasizing can equal.*
>
> "All the Way to Heaven,"
> *Elizabeth Sherrill*

Like Kit, we live in a land that isn't truly our home. We weren't meant to eke out a living from this soil. The ground is hard and parched. The air is toxic to our souls. We were made to breathe the air of heaven. The Spirit inside us resounds with our soul that this is true, and it breaks our hearts. Our home is elsewhere, and we long for that home.

As they wandered through the desert, the Israelites' souls longed for home. But in the early days, most of them believed their home was in Egypt, and they wanted to go back. They didn't realize their true home was the Promised Land, and, because of their lack of faith, they never entered it. Only their children would see it.

The Israelites never understood something very significant. Through all their desert wanderings, they never saw how God could use the sand, the heat, the lack of food and water and their irritable neighbors to grow them up. They continually ran back to Egypt in their hearts. They wanted the sure thing they could see and touch – a roof over their head and food in their belly. But God wanted to use that time in the sand to develop their trust in their savior. He wanted to use their circumstances to grow them. He didn't create the situation, but He wanted to use it to draw His people to Himself. All they had to do was allow Him to do so.

He wants to do the same with us. He wants to take all the circumstances of our lives, both great and terrible, and use them to draw us to Himself. He doesn't invent circumstances that lead to guilt, shame, fear and loss, but if we let Him, He will use them to strengthen our dependence on Him. Every awful thing that happens to us can be a tool in the Master Gardener's hand, a tool that will bring us closer to Him – a tool that will help us cross over to Him.

***

God made one promise to Israel long ago. He makes a new promise to us today. It's more than a promise of land we can map out and call ours. It's more than a place we must find. This promise saves us today and for eternity. The new promise is in Jesus – a promise that God is making a home with us.

Negotiating our way through this foreign land hasn't been easy, and for many of us it's been utterly tragic. But God nurtures us and tends us, preparing us to breathe Heaven's air. We can find rest for our souls knowing that He won't let us struggle in vain. And we can grow on this side of Heaven, because God Himself has crossed over to us.

> *The virgin will be with child and will give birth to a son, and they will call him Immanuel – which means, 'God with us.'*
>
> Matthew 1:23

# Write Your Story

**Day One – Wrapping Up**

Take some time for yourself. Get away and pore over these questions asking God to pull it all together for you. Ask Him to remind you of all you've done, all the crossings you've made. Acknowledge your hard work and celebrate!

1. Think back over the stories you've read in this study: the Samaritan woman, Peter on the water, Job, Lazarus' sisters Mary and Martha. Think back over your experiences with Jesus. By looking at how Jesus interacted with others, what do you learn about how He relates to you when you're hurting?

2. Like the woman who reached out to touch Jesus' robe, how can you reach out to Him and get help from Him when your heart is broken? What do you need from others when your heart is broken?

> *Oh Lord my God, I called to you for help and you healed me.*
>
> *Psalm 30:2*

## Day Two – Bringing it Together

1. What are the three most significant things you've learned from this study?

2. Is it possible God heals us and helps us grow even when we aren't aware of it? Have you ever realized, long after crying out for help, that God was actually mending your broken heart and helping you grow all along? What has God been doing in and for you behind the scenes?

> *"It was I who taught Ephraim to walk, taking them by the arms; but they did not realize it was I who healed them. I led them with cords of human kindness, with ties of love; I lifted the yoke from their neck and bent down to feed them."*
>
> *Hosea 11:3-4*

3. What crossings have you made? What crossings are you in the process of making? Tell someone about that and rejoice with God.

Take the time to thank God and others who have journeyed with you.

> *... to proclaim the year of the Lord's favor and the day of vengeance of our God, to comfort all who mourn and provide for those who grieve in Zion – to bestow on them a crown of beauty instead of ashes, the oil of gladness instead of mourning, and a garment of praise instead of a spirit of despair. They will be called oaks of righteousness, a planting of the Lord for the display of his splendor.*
> *Isaiah 61:2-3*

> *Jesus,*
> *Here I am. I need you. Tell me what's on your mind and in your heart. Tell me your dreams for me. I want to know. Let me tell you what's inside of me. Help me keep connecting with others after this study. Help me understand what I need from you and others and how to find that. And give me the courage to let you use my brokenness, my guilt, shame and fear to help others and bring honor to your name. Please use my whole life for your good work.*
> *Amen.*

**Group Discussion –** *What do you need as you wrap up this study?*
1. What are the three most significant things you've learned from this study?

2. As you think back through the stories you've read what did you learn about God's heart toward you when you're hurting?

3. Where is God when you're suffering?

4. What crossings have you made in the course of this study?

5. What do you need from God and others as you finish up?

# Afterword
# Home – The Promise of Heaven
# Write Your Story

*And I go back to Eden, in my mind, to imagine what it is going to be like for you and me in heaven. I suppose it will be a new and marvelous paradise, where love will exist in its purest form, where the beauty of diversity will be understood for the first time, where self-hatred will fade into an agreement with God about the splendor of His creation, where physical beauty will no longer be used as a commodity, where you and I will feel free in our sincere love for others, ourselves, and God. And I suppose it will be in heaven that you and I actually understand each other… all the arguments we had seeming so inconsequential, and the glory of God before us in all His majesty, shining like sunlight through our souls.*

*Donald Miller, "Searching For God Knows What"*

You've been reading stories of Jesus meeting real people in their suffering. You have a story of Jesus meeting you too. This study has been the story of you and God. Write your own afterword telling your story and God's story. When did the two stories collide? And where is the story going next?

# Biblical References

### Chapter 1: Crossings
12: "He uses pain for redemption…": Romans 8:28, Genesis 50:19.
12: The Israelites leave Egypt and wander in the desert: The Book of Exodus.

### Chapter 2: Broken Trust, Broken Heart
19: The disciples meet Jesus on the way to Emmaus: Luke 24:13-35.
21: "His primary motive in all things is love and redemption.":Exodus 34:6-7, Isaiah 30:18, Isaiah 61:1-3.

### Chapter 3: Knowing God's Heart Through His Word
29,30: Pharaoh chases the Israelites and they cross the sea: Exodus: 13-15.

### Chapter 4: Healing the Broken Heart Through Prayer
39: Hannah's story: 1 Samuel 1-2.

### Chapter 5: Guilt – Longing to be Known and Loved
49-50: The Samaritan woman: John 4:1-42.

### Chapter 6: Shame – Alienation that Breaks the Heart
64, 65: The sick woman: Mark 5:21-34.
65: "…Jesus referred to God as Abba Father…" Mark 14:36.

### Chapter 7: Fear – Losing Sight of His Presence
77, 78: Peter walks on water: Matthew 14:22-33.

### Chapter 8: When God Waits
91, 92: The death of Lazarus: John 11.

### Chapter 9: Home – The Promise of God With Us
102: Israel and the Promised Land: The Book of Exodus, Numbers 13-14.

# Further Study

God's plan for getting to know Him isn't a one-size-fits-all plan. He wired you up uniquely. Some will love to study and read for hours. Others will take a short verse and go out for a walk in God's creation. Still others will want to take a passage and discuss it with friends. Your job is to find how He designed you and run with it.

Here are some ways to know God better through the scriptures. If this is all new, experiment. Take one idea and work with it for a week. See how it goes.

- Pray to know God more deeply through His Word. He loves that request.

- Do word studies – choose a word like Father and look up in a concordance all the verses that speak of God as Father. Take notes!

- Read a Bible chapter or a few verses at a time – remember the point of reading the Bible is to get to know God and to transform your heart. It's not how much you read but how you develop a relationship with Jesus and act on what you read that counts.

- Study one of God's character traits, like compassion.

- Read the gospels or read through the whole Bible chronologically with a chronological Bible or online schedules. If you're new to the Bible, reading the gospel of John is a good place to begin.

- Do a Bible study with others so that, together, you can live out what you're learning and Jesus can love you through each other.

- Meditate on God's words. Carry cards with verses with you and read them through the day.

- Listen to teaching from the Word.

- Keep a journal of your insights and experiences with God.

- Memorize scripture. You'll see more clearly how your story and God's story come together when you have scripture memorized. Start small and build.

- Act on what you read in scripture. You'll forget it if it's left on the page. God brings scripture to life when you do what it says.

# Getting Support

A variety of supportive groups and individuals are out there. A couple of suggestions:

- Celebrate Recovery groups for help with habits, hang-ups and hurts
- Get recommendations for counselors/therapists in your area from a local church you trust
- Ask therapists about groups for specific issues
- Get into a small group through a local church

# Book Recommendations

I've read and treasured a number of books that have helped me along the way in my journey. Here are a few:

- Brother Lawrence and Frank Laubach, "Practicing His Presence"
- Brother Lawrence, "The Practice of the Presence of God" (including an essay on the life of Brother Lawrence by Joseph de Beaufort)
- Cowman, Mrs. Charles E., "Streams in the Desert"
- Cloud, Henry and John Townsend, "Boundaries," "Boundaries: The Workbook," "Changes That Heal" and "How People Grow"
- Eldredge, John, "The Sacred Romance," "The Sacred Romance Workbook and Journal," "Waking the Dead" and "Waking the Dead Workbook and Journal"
- Kreeft, Peter, "Making Sense Out of Suffering"
- Lewis, C.S., "The Problem of Pain" and "The Chronicles of Narnia"
- Miller, Donald, "Searching for God Knows What"
- Moore, Beth, "Praying God's Word"
- Seamands, David, "Healing for Damaged Emotions"
- Sherrill, Elizabeth, "All the Way to Heaven"
- Sittser, Gerald L., "A Grace Disguised"
- Smith, Hannah Whitall, "The Christian's Secret of a Happy Life"
- Yancey, Phillip, "Disappointment with God"

www.ingramcontent.com/pod-product-compliance
Lightning Source LLC
Chambersburg PA
CBHW050749100426
42744CB00012BA/1950